D0851434

Andersonville: The Southern Perspective

Copyright © 1995. J. H. Segars. All rights reserved. No part of this material may be reproduced in any form without written permissions from the publisher, except for brief reviews in periodicals.

Library of Congress Cataloging-in-Publication Data

Segars, J. H.
Andersonville: The Southern Perspective
ISBN 0-963-1963-4-1

95-068714
CIP

Andersonville: The Southern Perspective

Edited by J. H. Segars

Journal of Confederate History
Vol. XIII

Southern Heritage Press
P. O. Box 347163
Atlanta, Ga. 30334

Copyright 1995

As for you also, because of the blood of My covenant with you,
I have set your prisoners free from the waterless pit.

Return to the stronghold, O prisoners who have the hope;
This very day I am declaring that I will restore double to you.

Zechariah 9: 11, 12

CONTENTS

Prologue: Andersonville Revisited by J. H. Segars............................1

Acknowledgments...11

PART ONE
NARRATIVES FROM THE PAST

1. R. Randolph Stevenson: Andersonville Prison (1876)................15

2. Edward A. Pollard: The Exchange Question (1886)....................33

3. James Madison Page: The Dead Line and
    How the Raiders Were Executed (1908)....................................49

4. Edward W. Boate: A Federal Report (1866)................................69

5. Mildred Lewis Rutherford: Correspondence
    Regarding Henry Wirz, Commander of
    Andersonville Prison (1921)..79

PART TWO
CONTEMPORARY ANALYSIS

6. William R. Scaife: Andersonville and Sherman's
    Campaign for Georgia..99

7. Lee Joyner: Life in the Stockade...119

8. Mauriel Joslyn: The U. S. Policy of Retaliations on
    Confederate Prisoners of War...132

9. Wayne Dobson: All Were Prisoners There.................................147

10. Heinrich Wirz: A Response from the Wirz
    Family of Switzerland...161

11. Edwin C. Bearss: A Bibliography and
    Recommended Reading Guide...173

Epilogue: Who Caused Andersonville? by Mauriel Joslyn..............181

J. H. Segars

Prologue

Andersonville Revisited

J. H. Segars, a native of Eatonton, Georgia, is an administrator with the Georgia Department of Education in Atlanta. He is the author of *In Search of Confederate Ancestors: The Guide* and is currently co-editing with Charles Kelly Barrow a work entitled *The Forgotten Confederates: A Collection of Historical Accounts.*

Among the most disturbing scenes found in American history are the stark images of Union soldiers newly released from Andersonville. Those gaunt, malnourished prisoners of war—now displayed for posterity as if they were living skeletons in a carnival sideshow—continue to evoke feelings of utter shock, profound sadness, and bitter regret. Remembrances of this part of American history are painful. And though the story of Andersonville is greatly diminished by the passage of time, questions still remain: How could this national tragedy have happened? And who was to blame?

The very name of Andersonville brings to mind a place of infamy where thousands of emaciated captives lived and died in pitiful, inhuman conditions. But, beyond this, little else seems to be remembered: the collective memory of the nation has grown dim—almost to the point of amnesia. To southerners it appears that a national jury once convened, viewed a prostrate subject, and quickly pronounced a verdict of guilty—all on the testimony of select witnesses and without taking time to view the full scope of evidence. Too often it seems that this chapter of American history has been opened and shut, all in one swift motion.

Many of the details about this historical epoch are largely forgotten; even the official name of the prison—Camp Sumter—is no longer remembered. Confederate authorities chose the Andersonville site, along with others in the lower southeastern states, to relieve crowded facilities in and around Richmond. These new prison camps were far removed from the threat of cavalry raids and were situated near open rail lines. Moreover, the warmer climates would be beneficial to prisoner and guard alike and by relying on crops grown in the local area, hard-pressed Confederate military commissaries could be spared the additional burden of feeding captured Union soldiers. All in all, it seemed logical to construct military stockades in areas where natural resources were in abundance—especially timber and clear running streams. At any rate, the site selected near the tiny railroad crossing of Anderson Station in southwest Georgia appeared to be ideal for holding Union prisoners until they could be exchanged.

Andersonville is remembered for several reasons—principally the high death rate. The 26 1/2 acre open stockade was designed to hold no more than 8,000 to 10,000 men; yet, over 45,000 passed through the gates. Many of these men were already in a weakened condition upon arrival. In August of 1864, the inmate population rose to 32,000 and the death rate continued to climb. The most frequently mentioned reasons for the deaths included the following: scarcity of food, contaminated drinking water, inadequate shelter, lack of sewage control, an absence of essential medicines, the constant outbreak of diseases, and the overall stress of living in crowded, life-threatening conditions. All of this was a recipe for disaster. Even though the prison was only open for fourteen months, from February, 1864 to the end of the war in April, 1865, a total of 12,912 Union prisoners and approximately 250 Confederate guards perished.

Although other Civil War prisoner of war camps were guilty of similar living conditions and high death rates, Andersonville is the POW camp that remains notorious in the national memory. There is good reason for this—no other American POW camp received as much national publicity as Andersonville. Mrs. Peggy Sheppard, local historian and area resident since 1946, writes: "Even before the war ended, the Northern Press had started publishing sensational stories on the horrors of Andersonville." (*Andersonville, Georgia, USA*, 1973). And for over a century, sharp disagreement over the issues existed among the old veterans, newspaper editors, historians, and members of patriotic societies, in particular the United Daughters of the Confederacy and the Women's Relief Corps of the Grand Army of the Republic. Northern newspapers charged Southerners with gross mismanagement, intentional neglect, and purposeful cruelty. After the war, former Union prisoners published detailed narratives about their tribulations at Andersonville; understandably, most were bitter and partisan.

The national reporting was relentless. The U. S. War Department circulated photographs of emaciated prisoners which were reprinted over and over again in history texts. National publications such as *Harper's Weekly* continued to print critical articles and inflammatory illustrations. All of this had the same effect: people became aroused and public opinion began to form. Ultimately, after decades of Northern interpretations, Federal orthodoxy would become the official explanation for all that happened at Andersonville. Naturally, Southerners responded in defense but due to the lack of publishing resources, it was too little too late. The national war of words over Andersonville became another Confederate defeat. American history texts, the majority being published above the Mason-Dixon Line, had no further need for Southern viewpoints on this subject (or others as well).

Visitors to the present day site of the Andersonville prison and cemetery, located ten miles northeast of Americus on Georgia Highway 29, will encounter scenes in total contrast to those dismal days of 1864 and 1865. A serene and pastoral setting has replaced the scarred landscape where once stood a stench-filled stockade constructed of rough-hewn timbers and filled to the brim with desperate, dirty men. Today the National Park Service maintains 475 acres of beautiful and historic grounds. Congress authorized the Park Service to "provide an understanding of the overall prisoner of war

The Andersonville National Cemetery

story of the Civil War, to interpret the role of prisoner of war camps in history, to commemorate the sacrifice of Americans who lost their lives in such camps and to preserve the monuments located within the site." Thousands of headstones, closely aligned and properly maintained, cover the landscape, and the towering state monuments are most impressive. Two rolling hillsides descend into the stockade branch; Providence Spring, Confederate earthworks, escape tunnels, and well pits continue to be preserved on the stockade grounds. As the wind whistles through the distant Georgia pines and the sun begins to set, visitors begin to sense a feeling of uneasiness: they realize that this is a place of reverence and mystery.

For those intent on discovering the true story of Andersonville—the search will not be easy. This historical subject is submerged beneath layers of sensational reporting, strong sectional feelings, and continued disagreement over the issues. The basic understanding of the general public seems to be derived from historical fictions, and in particular from MacKinlay Kantor's Pulitzer Prize winning novel *Andersonville* (New York, 1955). Some of the books written by Union prisoners have amazing titles such as Robert H. Kellogg's *Life and*

Death in Rebel Prisons: Giving a Complete History of the Inhuman and Barbarous Treatment of Our Brave Soldiers by Rebel Authorities, Inflicting Terrible Suffering and Frightful Mortality, Principally at Andersonville, GA., and Florence, S. C., Describing Plans of Escape, Arrival of Prisoners, With Numerous and Varied Incidents and Anecdotes of Prison Life (Hartford, CT, 1965). If a detailed bibliographical list is viewed, from the titles alone it seems that all objectivity had been lost, and in many cases it has. Even the better written and most notable narratives must be scrutinized for historical accuracy. For example, John McElroy's *Andersonville: A Story of Rebel Prisons* (Toledo, 1879), long popular with Civil War researchers, is deemed to be "preposterously exaggerated" by noted historian Ovid L. Futch, author of *History of Andersonville Prison* (University of Florida Press, 1968). Moreover, this work is reviewed by the imminent scholar E. Merton Coulter as "utterly biased and fiercely hostile to all things Southern, with a haughty 'holier than thou' attitude at all times." Professor Coulter goes on to say that McElroy's "interest in pensions for Federal veterans explains why he wrote this book." (*Travels in the Confederate States*, Baton Rouge, 1948). Nevertheless, some of the prisoner narratives provide valuable information, especially John L. Ransom's *Andersonville Diary* (The Author, 1881) and John Maile's *Prison Life in Andersonville* (Los Angeles, 1912). And perhaps most surprising of all, some of the books by Union prisoners are essentially Southern viewpoints, in particular James Madison Page's *The True Story of Andersonville* (New York, 1908) and Herman A. Braun's *Andersonville: An Object Lesson on Protection* (Milwaukee, 1892).

A myriad assortment of writings can be found, but few are totally nonpartisan and most are written from the predominant Northern viewpoint. There remains a shortage of scholarly studies about American Civil War prisons, and especially about POW camps that operated in the North. One of the standard texts in use today is William B. Hesseltine's *Civil War Prisons: A Study in War Psychology* (Columbus, Ohio) which was first released in 1930. Fortunately, Civil War historians are beginning to focus on POW issues. William Marvel's *Andersonville: The Last Depot* (Chapel Hill, 1994), is a most welcomed addition to this area of study. As we dig into available sources about Andersonville, we encounter period writings which contain the lesser-known, minority viewpoints known principally as the "Southern Perspective." If these writings are validated and accepted as historically accurate, then the story of Andersonville takes on a different interpretation and meaning. For example, let's examine an eye-witness report by a Confederate nurse, Kate Cumming, so that we can capture a glimpse of the Southern mindset of the time. This excerpt is drawn from Miss Cumming's diary entitled *A Journal of Hospital Life in the Confederate Army of Tennessee From the Battle of Shiloh to the End of the War* (Louisville, 1866). The writer is traveling by train through Georgia and on August 19, 1864 she writes:

> Dr. Nagle and an officer who is stationed at Andersonville,where the prisoners are kept, spent the evening with us. The prisoners and their behavior was the principal topic of conversations, and from all we could learn we did not like the prospect of being so near them (Americus is ten miles below Andersonville). This officer informed us that no less than a hundred died daily. He said they were the most desperate set of men that he had ever seen. There were no parties among them, the black republicans and the copperheads, and they often have desperate fights, and kill each other. this officer said it was revolting to be near such men, and did not like his position.

> Dr. C. sent us to the depot on the 19th in an ambulance. The train stopped a little while at Fort Valley, where the Buckner and Gamble Hospitals, of our post, have remained. There we saw a few familiar faces. The train remained about half an hour at Andersonville, so we had time for a good view of the prisoner's quarters. I must say that my antipathy for prison-life any thing but removed by the sight. My heart sank within me at seeing so many human beings crowded so closely to-gether. I asked a gentlemen near why we had so many in one place. He answered that we would not have men enough to guard them were they scattered. O, how I thought of him who is the cause of all this woe on his fellow-countrymen Abraham Lincoln. What kind of heart can he have, to leave these poor wretches here? To think how often we have begged for exchange; but this unfeeling man knows what a terrible punishment it is for our men to be in Northern prisons, and how valuable every one of them is to us. For this reason he sacrifices thousands of his own. May heaven help us all!! But war is terrible.

For those unfamiliar with the "Southern Perspective" of Andersonville, these original observations might seem strange. Nevertheless, as we begin to explore different historical perspectives from material that we are not familiar with, questions begin to arise: Who was responsible for the breakdown of prisoner exchange between the United States and Confederate governments? Why didn't General Sherman send his entire force into Andersonville and free the Union prisoners? Did the Confederate authorities attempt to starve their Union captives? Did the United States government implement a policy of retaliation against Southern prisoners held in Northern POW camps? Was the camp commander, Henry Wirz, guilty of war crimes and his hanging justified? Were there "Andersonvilles" in the North? And perhaps the most important question of all—Could the whole tragedy of Andersonville have been lessened, or altogether avoided?

During the war, this area served as a train depot and supply center for thousands of Union soldiers who arrived by rail cars, were unloaded, and then marched to the nearby stockade. Today, the village of Andersonville is a destination for tourists. The narrow streets are filled with visitors who enjoy antique stores, specialty shops, Civil War reenactments, arts and craft exhibits, local restaurants, and a nineteenth century railroad depot currently used as a visitors center and museum. Several downtown buildings are of the 1860's era and in the center of town, directly in the middle of the main street, stands one of our nation's most controversial monuments—the memorial to Captain Henry Wirz, the last commander of the Andersonville stockade. Captain Wirz, a native of Switzerland and wounded veteran of the Fourth Louisiana Infantry, refused to implicate President Jefferson Davis for "atrocities" at the prison. Subsequently, a United States Military commission tried, convicted, and executed Wirz on November 10, 1865. But the irregularities in the trial to include bogus testimony from unreliable witnesses outraged many Southerners. After years of heated debate and national dialogue, the women of the Georgia Division, United Daughters of the Confederacy decided to take action by boldly commissioning a memorial to Captain Wirz. On May 12, 1909, a forty-five foot granite obelisk was unveiled before a passionate crowd of 4,000 Southerners. The old Confederate veterans, UDC delegates, state dignitaries, and area residents paid honor to their fallen comrade—the only Confederate official hung by the United States government following the war. The inscriptions appearing on the four sides of the memorial shaft, and long kept a secret, were unveiled to an incredulous world:

FRONT

In memory of Captain Wirz, C.S.A. Born Zurich, Switzerland, 1822. Sentenced to death and executed at Washington, D.C., Nov. 10, 1865.

'To rescue his name from the stigma attached to it by embittered prejudice, this shaft is erected by the Georgia Division, United Daughters of the Confederacy.'

SECOND SIDE

Discharging his duty with such humanity as the harsh circumstances of the times, and the policy of the foe permitted, Captain Wirz, became at last the victim of a misdirected popular clamor.

He was arrested in time of peace, while under the protection of a parole, tried by a military commission of a service to which he did not belong and condemned to ignominious death on charges of excessive cruelty to Federal prisoners. He indignantly spurned a pardon, proffered on condition that he would incriminate President Davis and thus exonerate himself from charges of which both were innocent.

THIRD SIDE

'It is hard on our men held in Southern prisons not to exchange them, but it is humanity to those left in the ranks to fight our battles. At this particular time to release all rebel prisoners North, would insure Sherman's defeat and would compromise our safety here.'

August 18, 1864
Ulysses S. Grant

FOURTH SIDE

'When time shall have softened passion and prejudice, when reason shall have stripped the mask of misrepresentation, the justice, holding even her scales, will require much of past censure and praise to change places."

December, 1888
Jefferson Davis

Wirz Monument, Village of Andersonville

Ironically, Captain Wirz is still honored by special ceremonies which are held in the small village of Andersonville each year. Those from outside the region might think it odd that Southerners continue to honor a man convicted as a war criminal over a century ago by the United States government. To many, however, Wirz remains the martyr. During these public ceremonies, tribute is paid by many: gray-clad reenactors, sophisticated ladies in period dress (some in black), local residents, and visitors from throughout the nation. In October of 1993 Henry Wirz's great-grandnephew, Colonel Heinrich L. Wirz, of Bremgarten, Switzerland and active military officer, arrived in Andersonville; he was scheduled to deliver a keynote address at his ancestor's memorial and to make appearances during the Andersonville Historic Fair weekend. During this special weekend, I had the privilege of meeting this gentleman and found his demeanor to be as imagined: soft-spoken, strong European accent (much like his ancestor, I supposed), a military profile, and manners typically Southern. Those in the crowd familiar with Southern history approached him with courtesy and due respect. Indeed, he was received with honor as the descendant of one who had paid the supreme sacrifice for the Cause—not as the scion of a Federal war criminal. Quite frankly, I'm not sure if JEB Stuart IV or any of the Lee family could have been treated any better on this particular day. But many of those in attendance were the descendants of Confederate soldiers, and some were linked to ancestors that served as Andersonville guards. Others descended from men who were prisoners in Northern POW camps; and a few had ancestors who suffered the same fate as many of the Union prisoners in Andersonville and are buried in   shallow graves near Northern POW camps.

After a while, I began to converse with Colonel Wirz and soon asked him a pointed question (one that I'm sure he had heard many times before): "After all these years, how does your family view the tragedy of Andersonville?" He smiled and in his noticeable Swiss accent, he remarked: "That is for the American people to decide." Somehow this was the response that I had expected. Later on, further explanation was provided in an article appearing in the November 2, 1993 edition of the *Americus Times-Recorder* as Colonel Wirz explained: "I believe in American justice that one day the stain on the family name would be removed." That was enough. This distinguished foreign visitor echoed a feeling strongly felt by many Southerners: that one day the whole episode of Andersonville would be properly revisited; that the stain upon Southern honor would be, if not totally removed, then lessened; that History would eventually identify all those responsible for this great American tragedy; and that healing would truly take place.

In the years since the War Between the States ended, many of the issues surrounding Andersonville were never really resolved in the minds of the American people. Southerners continued to be provoked by the charges of intentional starvation of Union prisoners, the refusal of prisoner exchange by General Grant, the Federal policy of retaliation against Confederate POWs, the questionable trial and execution of Henry Wirz by the U. S. government, and the years of "waving the bloody shirt" by partisan editors. For these reasons— and certainly others as well—the Southern Perspective endures. It is an important part of the Andersonville story. Hopefully, we will continue to search for historical truth no matter where it exists and truly learn from our national mistakes. And above all, may we continue to ask for the Mercy of Almighty God because, indeed, war is a terrible thing.

Pecan Lane entrance to Andersonville circa 1910.
Courtesy of the National Park Service.

ACKNOWLEDGMENTS

Southerners have long felt that the story of Andersonville should be properly retold, but with the inclusion of historical viewpoint and interpretation often omitted from traditional texts. To truly understand this interpretation, termed the "Southern Perspective," it seemed imperative that we include authoritative narratives written by those most familiar with the subject and who were close to Andersonville prison—in time and place. And while there are a number of reliable historians and period writers of the era, we chose to include some who are best known as staunch defenders of Confederate Andersonville. The following writers of the past were chosen for inclusion in this volume: Dr. R. Randolph Stevenson, Chief Surgeon of the Confederate hospitals at Andersonville; Edward A. Pollard and Mildred Lewis Rutherford, eminent Southern historians; and James Madison Page and Edward W. Boate, Union veterans who, after serving as prisoners in Andersonville, corroborated and upheld the Southern view.

The responsibility for interpreting the causes and effects of Andersonville has always been a burden for Southerners, and especially Georgians. Therefore, it seems most appropriate that the following native Georgians be called upon to provide contemporary analysis and interpretation: Mauriel Joslyn of Sparta, Bill Scaife of Atlanta, Lee Joyner of Monroe, Hank Segars of Lawrenceville, and Wayne Dobson of Macon.

We are indebted to the staff of the National Park Service at the Andersonville National Historic Site and Cemetery. Alan Marsh and Mike Jolly, park rangers and historical interpreters at Andersonville, and Charlene McCloud of the Atlanta Regional office, provided invaluable assistance. Special acknowledgment goes to Ed Bearss for allowing us to include his excellent Andersonville bibliography in this study. Incidentally, this was my opportunity to converse with Ed; he is truly interested in accommodating researchers and continues to be a great friend to the Civil War community.

There are a number of others who made contributions to this effort: Williard Rocker of the Washington Memorial Library of Macon, Georgia; John Sims, Andersonville historical researcher from Chattanooga, Tennessee; Gene Armistead of Escondido, California; the staff members of Georgia Department of Archives and History and the Georgia Department of Education Library in Atlanta; Peggy Sheppard and the Andersonville Guild; and my traveling companions, Scott Henry and Natalie Paige. Special thanks to my wife, Marie, for editorial assistance and for peaking my interest in Andersonville with stories about visiting the historic site as a teenager in the 1960's; the feelings of eeriness and overpowering silence that were encountered; and how she came upon the realization that this was sacred ground. After several visits to the cemetery and to the site of the old stockade, I fully concur with her evaluation.

Photographic acknowledgment and credits are as follows: the National Park Service Collection at Andersonville; the National Archives; the private collections of Lee Joyner, Charles D. Jones, Patrick Mines, Wayne Dobson, and Ricky Anthony Smith. George Whiteley, photography specialist with the Georgia Department of Archives and History, and Journal photographer Montgomery Hudson, and special acknowledgment to *Journal of Confederate History* typesetter Judy Daughtry of Stephen F. Austin State University in Nacogdoches, Texas.

And finally, I am indebted to Heinrich L. Wirz of Bremgarten, Switzerland. The Wirz family originated in Zurich and they trace their ancestry to 1422. I had the good fortune to meet Colonel Wirz in the village of Andersonville in 1993, and to subsequently converse several times back and forth between Georgia and Switzerland. His insight underscores what generations of Southerners have always felt about the events surrounding Andersonville.

This volume is dedicated to the descendants of the Confederate guards at Andersonville, to the members of the Wirz family, and to the people of Sumter and Macon Counties, Georgia.

Part One

Narratives From the Past

R. Randolph Stevenson

Chapter One

Andersonville Prison (1876)

Dr. R. Randolph Stevenson served as Chief Surgeon of the
Confederate States Military Hospitals at the Andersonville and
authored *The Southern Side; Or, Andersonville Prison* in 1876.
This book, published by the Turnbull Brothers of Baltimore, is
an eye-witness account of historical events at Camp Sumter.
Dr. Stevenson's valuable recapitulation of Union deaths by
causes, months, and states of residency is included at the end
of this selection.

Andersonville, before the war, was an insignificant station on the Southwestern Railroad, in Sumter County, Georgia. It is about sixty miles from Macon, and ten miles from Americus, the shire town of the county. Its latitude is 32° 10' N.; longitude 85° W. from Washington. The climate is mild, and subject to no great extremes of heat and cold; the mean annual range of the thermometer being about 60° Fahrenheit. The following scientific report of this place, made to the author by Prof. Jones, will more fully explain the general character of the country, soil, water, &c.

Camp Sumter, Andersonville, Ga.,
September 23d, 1864

Surgeon R. R. Stevenson,
    In Charge of Confederate States Military Prison Hospitals, Andersonville, Ga.

Sir:—In accordance with your request that I should furnish you with the general results of my observations upon the medical topography of Andersonville, the following facts are presented. The surgeon in charge of the Confederate States Military Prison Hospitals will please excuse the brevity and imperfections of this communication, as my duties and labors have been such that I have had but an hour or two to devote to its preparation.

GENERAL VIEW OF THE MEDICAL TOPOGRAPHY OF ANDERSONVILLE AND THE COUNTRY IN THE IMMEDIATE VICINITY.

Elevation of the Country.—The country is rolling, and is elevated between three and four hundred feet above the level of the sea. The hills vary in height from forty to one hundred and twenty feet above the level of the water-courses. The summit of the hill upon which the Confederate States General Hospital is situated is elevated one hundred and eight feet above the branch of Sweet Water Creek, which flows at its base. The railroad station is elevated about sixty-six feet above the level of this branch of Sweet Water Creek.

Character of the Soil.—The surface soil is sandy, with but little vegetable mould. For agricultural purposes the soil of this immediate locality may be characterized as light sandy soil; many of the hills which have been cleared and washed by the rains present a red appearance, from the presence of oxide of iron. The hills are composed of alternate layers of sand and pipe-clay, commonly called soap-stone. Both the sand and clay present various colors, from pure white to deep red.

Geological Position.—I have as yet discovered no fossils by which the geological position of this region may with certainty be determined. As far, however, as my knowledge of the country lying above and below extends, this region should be referred to the Tertiary; or more exactly, to the upper or burrh stone strata of the Eocene formation.

Character of Water.—I have carefully analysed the waters from various localities, and find them all remarkably pure; the waters of the wells and of the small streams do not differ to any great extent in specific gravity from that of distilled water, and they contain only mere traces of the chlorides and sulphates, and of the salts of lime, magnesia and iron. The well upon the summit of the hill near your headquarters is of remarkable purity, and in fact it may be considered as equal in purity to the purest well-water in the world. The temperature, 18° C., is sufficiently cool in this climate to render it refreshing. The waters of the branches of Sweet Water Creek are equally pure, with the exception of the presence of minute quantities of vegetable matter; these do not however exist in sufficient quantity to be of the slightest moment in a medical point of view. The waters of these creeks are not so pleasant as the well-water, because their temperature is several degrees higher, and subject to considerable variations according to the volume and rapidity of the current and the degree of external heat. I think that we are justified, from this examination of the water of Andersonville, in the conclusion that little or no lime exists in the soil.

I have also carefully examined the waters within the stockade and hospital, and find them to be of remarkable purity. The water of the stream that enters the stockade, as well as of the bold spring which mingles its waters with the stream just after its entrance into the stockade, and which are extensively used by the prisoners for drinking and cooking, is of great purity, containing only traces of the sulphates, chlorides, and salts of lime, iron and magnesia. The same is true of the water of the stream which enters the hospital enclosure, as well as of the deep wells with in the hospital grounds.

Vegetation.—The forest-trees covering the high grounds consist chiefly of the long-leaf pine (*Pinus Australis*), yellow or two-leaved pine (*P. Mitis*), barren scrub oak (*Quereus Catesbai*), red oak (*Q. Rubra*), Spanish oak, black oak, post oak (*Q. Obtusiloba*), upland willow oak (*Q. Phellos*), wild plum, persimmon (*Diospyros Virginiana*), chinquapin, and other small shrubs, as the whortleberry, haw, sweet leaf, &c. The swamps are clothed chiefly with black gum (*Nyssa Grandidentata*), tupelo (*N. Aquatica, N. Sylvatica*), sweet gum (*Liquidambar Styraciflua*), red flowery maple (*Aeer Rubrum*), small magnolia (*Magnolia Glauca*), red bay (*Laurus Cerasus*), and numerous shrubs characteristic of this region.

From this examination we conclude that there is no recognizable source of disease in the waters and soil of Andersonville.

I hope to be able in future to communicate my views more fully upon the soil and climate, when I shall have more time at my command. In conclusion, allow me to return my thanks for the prompt and efficient assistance which you have so cheerfully and courteously rendered me in my "pathological investigations," ordered by the Surgeon-general.

> Very respectfully, your obedient servant,
> Joseph Jones,
> Surgeon P.A.C.S.

After repeated efforts by the Confederate States Government to effect a general exchange of prisoners, it was determined to locate a large prison in Southwest Georgia. Andersonville was the site selected, for various humane considerations: first, its superiority over Richmond, Va., in obtaining supplies of food, water and timber, "in the immediate neighborhood of saw and grist mills," and the advantage of a warmer climate. These important considerations, connected with the fact that Richmond was constantly exposed to raiding parties by the enemy, were the principal causes of the removal of the prisoners to Andersonville. Captain W.W. Winder, a son of General John H. Winder, who was afterwards made chief in command of all the prisons and prisoners east of the Mississippi River, was dispatched from Richmond with orders to secure the location of a prison in this portion of Georgia. Andersonville was the site selected, and in due course of time a stockade was built here for the accommodation of ten thousand prisoners.

It was constructed by planting large pickets five feet in the ground, and projecting above the surface some twenty feet in height. This enclosure contained at first about twenty acres; afterwards, to meet the daily increasing number of prisoners, it was enlarged to thirty acres. Surrounding this were two outer lines of pickets, the outer one at a distance of one hundred and eighty feet from the main line. These lines were not so high as the inner or first line, being twelve and sixteen feet respectively. These lines were intended as a means of defence and offence, while they also prevented the prisoners from tunnelling out.

A work of the size of this prison was completed by no ordinary means. General Howell Cobb, who was at this time commanding the

Anderson Station, 1995.

militia districts of Georgia and Florida, ordered the impressment of some five or six hundred negroes to assist in the work, thereby greatly facilitating its progress.

The shape of the prison was that of a parallelogram. A bold stream of water ran westward through the enclosure, and from the edge of the stream to the brow of the hill on each side was a gradual inclined plane. The camp inside of the prison presented two hill-sides, one facing the north and the other the south. A strong dam was erected at the upper side of the stockade, in order to give the water below an increased velocity. This stream along the entire course of the stockade was a boxed canal, the upper part being used for bathing purposes and the lower portion as a privy. This was an admirable arrangement; and if it had not been that the fortunes of war crowded the prisoners to this post, producing the direful effects of an unforeseen pestilence, a better selection could not have been made in this part of the South for the health and comfort of the captives. At each angle of the prison was a small fort, only one of which had mounted guns; these, with the outer lines of pickets and rifle-pits in echelon, completed the works of offence and defence. Along the inner line of pickets, sentry-boxes were placed at regular intervals for the guards. Large fires were kept up on dark nights, to aid the sentries in detecting those who might attempt to escape.

On the inside of the prison, about twenty feet from the picket-lines, was the "dead line;" this was a barrier employed in the discipline of prisons both North and South to prevent the prisoners from escaping; it was made by driving stakes securely into the ground, with pieces of timer nailed along the top of the stakes, the whole being about five feet high. (The arrangement as described was perhaps peculiar to Andersonville or other Southern prisons. It would appear, indeed, that in many of the prisons of the North (notable Fort Delaware and Point Lookout) the "dead line" was almost as imaginary as a line of latitude or longitude, and the unfortunate captives not expert in prison geography were liable to be shot down at any moment at the whim of the sentry, while entirely unconscious of having trespassed upon a "line" which they could not see.)

The camp on each side of the stream was laid off in regular streets running at right angles, experience having taught those in charge of prisoners that close barracks in a warm climate would breed disease. A number of sheds were erected to protect the prisoners from the inclemency of the weather. As the prisoners were constantly arriving by thousands before the interior arrangements were complete, they were instructed to improvise temporary coverings from the timer already in the stockade, until suitable winter-quarters could be provided for them. These were made in various ways; some were of plank, some tents, some thatched cottages, some adobe huts, some brush arbors, presenting a miniature city, grotesque in appearance and singular in its construction. It was amusing to observe in this camp of from ten to thirty thousand prisoners, the alacrity with which thousands of them would enter into speculation, or "dickering" as they called it. There were groceries, restaurants, sutlers, merchants, brokers, bakers, wood-dealers, and even land-jobbers engaged in buying and selling ten or twenty feet square of land. The ground occupied by the prison was at first almost covered with pine-stamps, the timber having been used for the construction of the prison and temporary shelters. These stumps were all dug up by the prisoners for lightwood, and the vivid light derived from this "fat pine," as it is termed in the South, enlivened many a game of "euchre" and "seven-up." All classes of men were represented here, the honest ploughboy and the city ruffian: Jew and Christian, men of every tongue, race and nativity, were enclosed in this one prison. The men became apparently reckless, I might say thoroughly brutalized by long confinement and deferred hopes of exchange; they seemed to become indifferent to the ordinary decencies of life, and many of them grew as filthy and disgusting in their habits as are the insane or idiotic with whom there is no sense of shame or moral restraint. Here too moral restraints generally lost their force, and the worst passions of the worst men began to assert themselves unchecked; murders and robberies were of frequent occurrence, and so reckless had a portion of the prisoners become, that the more humane among them petitioned General Winder for leave to try the offenders by a court-martial chosen from their own number. This being granted, they proceeded to try the offenders, and the result was that six of their number were found guilty by their comrades of murder, and were hung on a gallows inside the stockade, in the presence of the assembled prisoners. This checked the evil to some extent.

On the north side of the prison, good and substantial barrack accommodations were begun, and the sheds were nearly completed when the work was stopped on account of prison gangrene and scurvy attacking the prisoners, resulting in such great mortality that the post was afterwards abandoned, that is, for the regular reception of prisoners. The prison had two gates, one for egress and the other for ingress. Several bold springs of pure water emerged from the north bank of the stream, and numerous wells of pure water existed inside of the prison. Many of the prisoners lost their lives in attempting to tunnel out of the prison from secret passages that led from these wells. In consequence of the outer line of pickets, tunnelling was in most instances a failure. I remember one poor fellow was permitted to make his tunnel, as he thought, a success. The reader can imagine his chagrin when he came to the top of the ground and found himself confronted by another line of pickets.

On the outer side of the prison, and near the place of ingress, was the baking and cook house. In this place a part of the rations was cooked; the rest was done inside of the stockade by the prisoners. The rations were issued to the prisoners, guards and attendants, regularly once a day; occasionally some of the prisoners would be put on a half-rations for some misdemeanor. The rations furnished to the prisoners and Confederate troops on duty there were the same in quantity and quality: all fared alike. The first prisoners that were brought to this post, March 1, 1864, were a motley crew of eight hundred and fifty foreigners, under the name of Federal troops from the New England States. Their petitions for exchange to the Government that had entrapped them into its service had fallen upon deaf ears. Their long prison-life told fearfully upon them; home-sickness and hopes deferred had borne them down altogether. They were marched off to their new prison, and soon made themselves tolerably comfortable. Colonel A.W. Persons, of Fort Valley, Ga., had temporary command of the post at this time, a small detachment of Confederate troops in his movement toward Atlanta, engaging the enemy almost every day for three months, was adding thousands of prisoners to the already crowded post of Andersonville. The prisoners from this source—the Army of the Tennessee—were usually received when no provision had been made for them; the results of the battle-field being, of course, beyond the prevision of man. Thousands of them would at times arrive shortly after the telegrams announcing their capture. Under these circumstances it was impossible to be fully prepared to receive them. It will also be observed that by the first of May, 1864, the prison was taxed to its fullest extent, viz. for the reception of 10,000 men.

The enlargement of the prison from its original dimensions was thought to be of sufficient capacity to receive all the prisoners that would possibly be sent here. It may be asked, why were the prisoners sent from Richmond to this post when it was in a crowded condition? The fact is that General Lee's army at this time were living on short rations; not so much in consequence of a scarcity of provisions in the Confederacy, as the difficulty in transporting the supplies. At this time there was only one line of communication from the southern portion of the Confederate States to Richmond, and that was over the North Carolina Railroad, via Danville, Va. Under these circumstances the relief consequent upon the removal of ten or twenty thousand men from the scene of General Lee's operations can be readily understood. Self-preservation is the first law of nature, for communi-

View of stockade grounds toward sinks and spring branch;
replica of stockade wall in left background.

ties as well as individuals, and the removal of the prisoners to Andersonville was the only alternative, particularly as the Confederate Commissioner of Exchange (Colonel Ould) could not, through the obstinacy of the Federal Government, effect an exchange, as will be shown by official documents in another part of this work. The object in the removal of the prisoners was in the interest of humanity, however disastrous the results may have afterwards proved.

About the middle of May gangrene and scurvy began to make their appearance, and by the 20th of June these diseases had reached to such a point that General Winder (who did not arrive there until the 17th day of June, 1864) deemed it expedient to remove the prisoners to other points immediately, thereby seeking to abate the pestilence by dividing them into smaller posts. It must not be imagined that even at this late date many unforeseen difficulties had to be overcome. The few remaining railroads of the South were taxed to their utmost extent, and there was great difficulty in obtaining transportation. Barrack accommodations had to be built; supplies were to be collected; all these things had to be done before the prisoners could be removed. As soon as all the preliminaries were arranged, General Winder received orders to remove the prisoners to Millen and other points, as he might deem most suitable for their health, comfort and safety. About this time the Federal Government, knowing the straitened circumstances afterwards proved, with no idea of carrying out the provisions of the cartel, but simply to balk and frustrate the designs of the Confederate Government in making suitable provisions to take care of the captives for any length of time.

About the 25th of July, 1864, General Winder made a report to the War Department at Richmond, stating fully the condition of the prisoners, and recommending, first, the removal of at least 20,000 to other points remote from Andersonville; second, that the barracks or sheds already commenced should be completed, as they could be used for hospital purposes; third, that a number of disabled soldiers be detailed to raise vegetables for the prisoners, since they needed these as well as medicines; that until this could be done, a suitable number of agents be permitted to travel through the country by railroad to procure vegetables &c.; fourth, that hospital accommodations should be erected outside the prison. This report was sent to the War Department at Richmond, and the suggestions were sanctioned. They were carried out almost to the letter in some instances, as will be shown by official documents in another part of this work. By the last of September 1864 all the prisoners, except 5000 not able to bear transportation, were removed from Andersonville, and it virtually ceased to be a post for the reception of prisoners. Still, inasmuch as the Government had expended a large amount of money and devoted much time to render it a suitable place for a prison, it was not deemed advisable to abandon it altogether, and the place was therefore put in process of renovation. By the carelessness of the prisoners in the use of the sinks over the boxed canal, this had become a nuisance. To remedy this it was covered with sand and lime and the channel enlarged; the dam was improved, and the passage for the water at the lower side of the prison widened, so as to give the water free exit. The barracks and cook-house were enlarged, and the hospital buildings outside the prison were begun. General Jno. H. Winder, with his staff, composed of Capt. W.W. Winder, A.A.G., Capt. R.B. Winder, A.Q.M., and Surgeon J.H. White, proceeded with the prisoners to Millen, Georgia. They remained there, however, but a short time, the approach of Gen. Sherman's army forcing them to remove their prisoners to Florence, S.C.

As before mentioned, none but the sick and wounded, together with the attendants, nurses and medical officers, and a small guard, were left at Andersonville. The post was now placed in command of Colonel Gibbs, with R.B. Thomas, A.A.G., Major G.M. Proctor, and Capt. J.W. Armstrong had charge of the commissary department. Capt. Henry Wirz had the same control over the discipline of the hospital that he had formerly held over the prison; Surgeon R.R. Stevenson was placed in chief control of the medical department, with some thirty assistant-surgeons and contract-doctors. The process of renovating the post was now pushed on with vigor and rapidity, considering the small force and limited means at the command of Captain Wirz. In a short time the whole premises were in a much improved condition, and the chances of the sick were growing more hopeful. At one time it had been thought by the medical officers of the post that nearly all the infected would die, but by the use of vegetables in such quantities as could be procured, and an acid beer made from corn-meal and sorghum molasses, the death-rate fell from about 3000 in August to 100 for the month of December.

A temporary hospital had been improvised by Surgeon J.H. White, and established outside of the prison enclosure. This was done when gangrene and scurvy appeared in the stockade; but it was still inadequate to receive all the infected sick, and four hundred and fifty-one of these died in the prison. This temporary hosptial was similar to the ordinary field-hospital improvised after a great battle. It covered about five acres of ground, was well shaded and watered, and stood between two water-courses, upon a promontory of land sloping in two different directions. It was enclosed by a plank fence, and supplied with tents and tent-flies. Sometimes as many as 2500 prisoners would be in this enclosure. Of this number 2000 would be on the sick-list, and the remainder, convalescents, cooks, nurses, &c., were paroled to a certain limit around the hospital grounds, in order to give them the advantage of looking after the comfort of their sick comrades, in the way of getting wood, pine-boughs, straw, &c. A great many of these men violated their paroles and left their dying comrades, afterwards to appear on the witness-stand to give evidence against those who had befriended them whilst they were in prison.

The rules and regulations of the hospital were posted up in conspicuous places; the roll was called twice a day; the men were divided into squads of ninety and messes of fifteen men, in the same manner that had been practised in the prison. The squads were under the charge of a sergeant, who was held responsible for the good conduct of his company. The hospital was divided into four divisions, each under the charge of a medical officer, who was responsible to the chief surgeon—at first Surgeon J.H. White, after him Surgeon R.R. Stevenson, and lastly Surgeon Clayton. The rations and medicines issued to the prisoners in both the prison and hospital were of the same kind and quantity that were issued to the Confederate troops.

Strenuous efforts were made by the writer to have the hospital-sheds built as suggested by him in his report to the Surgeon-general. It was proposed to erect forty sheds, twenty feet wide by one hundred feet in length, eight feet high at the caves, with a space of thirty feet between them, each shed capable of containing from twenty to forty patients. The sides of the sheds were covered with awnings, to be raised or lowered at pleasure for ventilation, which the sick in a warm climate so much need. These buildings were nearly all completed, and were standing at the end of the war as a monument to the intentions of their builders.

The dead were buried about a half-mile to the northwest of the prison. They were placed side by side in long trenches, and well covered up. Each grave was carefully marked by a stake bearing a number corresponding with that on the hospital register, which gave the name, rank, regiment, company, and disease of the patient. Among the Confederate surgeons there were some who remained by their dying patients when even their own countrymen had deserted them, and who carefully preserved the long death-rolls for the benefit of those who at some future day might wish to know the last resting-place of their comrades and friends. Some of these devoted men died at their posts; and perhaps a day may come when in this city of the dead a memorial shall be raised to commemorate their fidelity to their calling and to humanity.

Every comfort was provided for the sick and wounded that could be obtained within the limited means of the Confederate Government. Nothing more strikingly shows the great resources of the Southern country than the fact that it fed its own soldiers in the field, its citizens, the prisoners, and almost fed the hosts of Grant and Sherman;

Serving rations by squad. Original illustration
by Walton Taber from *Century Magazine*, July, 1890.
Courtesy of the National Park Service.

and notwithstanding the destruction of railroads, supplies, mills, factories, farming implements, &c., by Federal raiders, cases of actual suffering for food on the part of soldiers, citizens, and prisoners, were seldom witnessed until near the close of the war.

It is useless at this point for me to go into a minute detail of the remote cause of the miseries and sufferings that occurred here, as this will be sufficiently shown by various official records in another part of this work. I may, however, mention that diarrhea, dysentery, scurvy, and gangrene were the principal diseases of which the prisoner died. These maladies arose mainly from a want of that diet to which the Northern soldiers had been accustomed. The quantity was quite sufficient to sustain life, but the bread was made from cornmeal, and not from wheaten flour. This produced diarrhea, and hence laid the foundation of all those symptoms resulting from defective nutrition. To this may be added the moral degradation of the prisoners themselves, as was shown by their filthy habits and defective hygienic regulations. Almost every prisoner that paid a strict regard to personal cleanliness escaped the pestilence. Disappointment and despondency in regard to exchanges seem to have been the most potent cause in lowering the vitality of mind and body and predisposing the men to disease. In corroboration of this fact I will mention that Dr. Joseph Jones, who was ordered to Andersonville by the Surgeon-general for the purpose of making certain "pathological investigations on the cadaver," says in his report to the Surgeon-general:— "Surrounded by these depressing agencies, the postponement of the general exchange of prisoners, and the constantly receding hopes of deliverance, through the action of their own Government, depressed the already desponding spirits, and destroyed those mental and moral energies so necessary for a successful struggle against disease and its agents. Home-sickness and disappointment, mental depression and distress, attending the daily longings for an apparently hopeless release, appeared to be as potent agencies in the destruction of these prisoners as the physical causes of actual diseases."

At one time there were nearly 8000 sick prisoners in the prison and hospital, and the mortality was very great during the months of July, August, and September, 1864, notwithstanding all possible efforts were made by the surgeons as well as the officers of the post to check its ravages. The greatest difficulty was experienced in procuring medicines and antiscorbutics. These were made contraband of war by an order of the Federal Government, and the most rigid discipline failed to make the prisoners pay that attention to cleanliness which was absolutely necessary. The medical corps was altogether insufficient in numbers to attend to the vast amount of patients, and it was impossible to procure medical assistance. The cooks, nurses, and attendants were drawn from paroled prisoners, and many of these abandoned their trust and made their escape on the first opportunity that presented, leaving their sick and dying comrades to perish. The guards on duty here were similarly affected with gangrene and scurvy. Captain Wirz had gangrene in an old wound which he had received in the battle of Manassas in 1861, and was absent from the Post some four weeks on surgeon's certificate. (In his trial, certain Federal witnesses swore to his killing certain prisoners in August 1864, when he (Wirz) was actually absent on sick leave in Augusta, Ga., at the time.) General Winder had gangrene of the face, and was forbidden by his surgeon, J.H. White, to go inside the stockade. Colonel G.C. Gibbs, commandant of the post, had gangrene of the face, and was furloughed under the medical certificate of surgeons Wible and Gore, of Americus, Ga. The writer of these pages can fully attest the effects of gangrene and scurvy, contracted while on duty there; their marks will follow him to his grave. The Confederate graveyard at Andersonville will fully prove that the mortality among the guards was almost as great in proportion to the number of men as among the Federals. For a period of some three months (July, August, and

September, 1864), Captain Wirz and the few faithful medical officers of the post were engaged night and day in ministering to the wants of the sick and dying, and caring for the dead. So arduous were their duties that many of the medical officers were taken sick and had to abandon their post. In fact, the pestilence assumed such fearful proportions, that Medical Director S.H. Stout could scarcely induce such medical men as could be spared from the pressing wants of the service (Georgia was at this time one vast hospital) to go to Andersonville.

It was this horrible condition of affairs at Andersonville and other prison-posts that prompted Colonel Ould, the Confederate Commissioner of Exchange, to make his repeated efforts in the interest of humanity to get the Federal Government (as they had refused all further exchanges) to send medicines, supplies of clothing, &c. (offering to pay for them in gold or cotton), for the exclusive use of the Federal prisoners, to be dispensed, if desired, by Federal surgeons sent for that purpose. The same motives prompted the President and Vice-president of the Confederate States to make the proposal to parole and send them home, although they were the only hostages held for a like number of suffering Confederate prisoners held at the North. These facts cannot be denied or explained away. Writers for effect may descant on "rebel barbarity," and present to a horrified world the photographs of diseased and emaciated wretches as proof of their charges; but the fact remains that the authorities at Washington, by obstinately refusing to listen to the liberal and repeated proposals of the Confederate Government, were the real authors of most of this misery and death.

Thirteen thousand men lie buried in the graveyard at Andersonville. When the web of falsehood, concealment and perjury called "the Wirz trial" shall be rent, and the truth known, it will be seen that the real responsibility lies with the men who sacrificed these poor wretches to their own ambition.

APPENDIX

RECAPITULATION OF DEATHS BY STATES.

ALABAMA	15	NEW JERSEY	170
CONNECTICUT	315	NEW YORK	2572
DELAWARE	45	NORTH CAROLINA	17
DIST. OF COLUMBIA	14	OHIO	1030
ILLINOIS	850	PENNSYLVANIA 1811	
INDIANA	504	RHODE ISLAND 74	
IOWA	174	TENNESSEE	738
KANSAS	5	VERMONT	212
KENTUCKY	436	VIRGINIA	288
LOUISIANA	1	WISCONSIN	244
MAINE	233	U.S. ARMY	399
MARYLAND	194	U.S. NAVY	100
MASSACHUSETTS	768	Citizens, Teamsters	
MINNESOTA	79	&c.	166
MICHIGAN	630	Men that were Hung	
MISSOURI	97	by the Prisoners	6
NEW HAMPSHIRE	124	Unknown U.S.	
Died in Small		Soldiers	443
Pox Hospital	68		

Total   12,912

The following exhibit, as collated from the Hospital Register and Prison Records, will be found to be as correct as any yet published:

Total number of Prisoners on hand at end of

April, 1864	10,427	November, 1864	1,359
May, 1864	13,454	December, 1864	4,706
June, 1864	23,307	January, 1865	5,046
July, 1864	31,678	February, 1865	5,851
August, 1864	31,693	March, 1865	3,319
September, 1864	8,218	April, 1865	51
October, 1864	4,208		

Deaths in Stockade and Hospital during the Existence of the Prison.

March, 1864	283	October, 1864	4,590
April, 1864	576	November, 1864	492
May, 1864	703	December, 1864	160
June, 1864	1201	January, 1865	100
July, 1864	1317	February, 1865	139
August, 1864	3076	March, 1865	192
September, 1864	2794	April, 1865	32

Total   12,912

The greater number of deaths in September and October, in proportion to the number in prison, will be explained by the fact that all the well men were removed from Andersonville in these months, and none were left except the sick and wounded.

Day and date of greatest number of Prisoners at Andersonville—33,114—August 8th, 1864.

Day and date of greatest number of deaths, August 23d, 1864, 127.

Number of Prisoners received during its occupation, 45,613.

Daily average of deaths during its occupation, 29 3/4.

Ratio of mortality per 1000 of mean strength, 24 per cent.

Mortality of 18,000 registered patients, 75 per cent.

The Diseases of which the Prisoners died will be found in the following classifications:

Anasarca	377	Hydrocele	1
Asphyxia	7	Hemorrhoids	1
Ascites	24	Jaundice	9
Asthma	3	Laryngitis	4
Bronchitis	93	Nostalgia	7
Catarrh	55	Nephritis	4
Constipation	5	Phthisis	137
Diarrhea, Chronic	4000	Pleuritis	54
Diarrhea, Acute	817	Pneumonia	321
Debilitas	198	Paralysis	1
Diphtheria	3	Rheumatism	83
Dyspepsia	2	Scurvy	3574
Diabetes	1	Syphilis	7
Dysenteria	1384	Scrofula	3
Erysipelas	11	Stricture	1
Febris Typhoides	229	Sunstroke	52
Fistula	2	Small Pox	68
Fracture	1	Vaccine Ulcers	4
Febris Remittens	177	Gunshot Wounds	155
Gonorrhea	3	Unknown	443
Gangrene	678	Hung in Stockade	6

Total   12,912

PLAN OF THE ANDERSONVILLE PRISON.

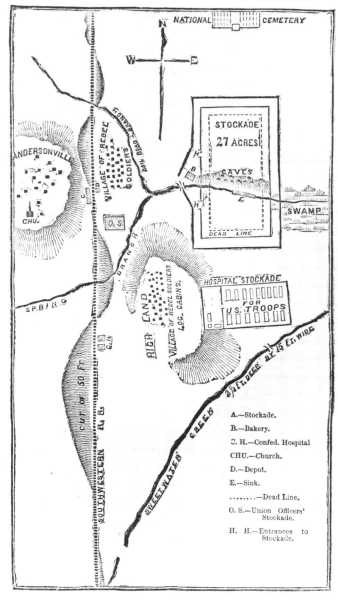

Map appearing on the front page of the *New York Times*,
November 26, 1865. Courtesy of the Joyner Collection,
George S. Whiteley IV, photographer.

Edward A. Pollard

Chapter Two

A Confederate Report (1886)

Edward Alfred Pollard was the distinguished editor of the *Daily Richmond Examiner* from 1861 to 1867. This selection is drawn from Pollard's monumental Confederate history *The Lost Cause,* originally published in 1866, and now considered a classic by many Southerners. Reprints of this 752 page book are available from Gramercy Books, distributed by Outlet Book Company, Inc., a Random House Company, 40 Englehard Avenue, Avenel, New Jersey 07001.

The exchange of prisoners taken during the war; their treatment in their places of confinement North and South; the incidents of the cartel, altogether, constitute so large and interesting a subject that we have reserved its treatment for a separate chapter. On the exposition of this intricate matter depends much of the good name of the Confederates and the contrary title of the enemy; and it may be remarked that no subject which tended to keep alive a feeling of bitterness and animosity between the Northern and Southern people was more effective than recrimination about the cartel, and the alleged cruelty to prisoners of war on both sides. The exposition we propose to make is mainly by a chain of records, extending through the war, thus best securing authenticity of statement, and combining these documents in a unity of narrative, so as to place before the reader a complete view and a severe analysis of the whole subject.

In the first periods of the war, and with the prospect of its early termination, but little account was taken of prisoners captured on either side. Indeed, some time elapsed at Washington before any lists were kept of these captures; and after the first remarkable battle of the war, that of Manassas, in 1861, it was actually proposed (by Mr. Boyce of South Carolina), in the Provisional Congress at Richmond, to send back the Federal prisoners taken on that field without any formality whatever. The Fort Donelson capture, however, appeared to have developed for the first time the value and interest of the exchange question, and was the occasion of remarkable perfidy on the part of the Washington authorities.

Just previous to these important captures, Gen. Wool, on the Federal side, had declared, in a letter dated the 13th February, 1862: "I am alone *clothed with full power*, for the purpose of arranging for the exchange of prisoners," and had invited a conference on the subject. Gen. Howell Cobb, on the part of the Confederacy, was appointed to negotiate with him; and the two officers decided upon a cartel by which prisoners taken on either side should be paroled within ten days after their capture, and delivered on the frontier of their own country. The only point of tenacious difference between them was as to a provision requiring each party to pay the expense of transporting their prisoners to the frontier; and this point Gen. Wool promised to refer to the decision of his Government. At a second interview on the 1st March, Gen. Wool declared that his Government would not consent to pay these expenses; when Gen. Cobb promptly gave up the point, leaving the cartel free from all of Gen. Wool's objections, and just what he had proposed in his letter of the 13th February. Upon this, Gen. Wool informed Gen. Cobb that "his Government had changed his instructions," and abruptly broke off the negotiation. The occasion of this bad faith and dishonour on the part of the enemy was, that in the interval they had taken several thousand prisoners at Fort Donelson, which reversed the former state of things, and gave them a surplus of prisoners, who, instead of being returned on parole, were carried into the interiour, and incarcerated with every circumstance of indignity.

In the second year of the war a distinct understanding was obtained on the subject of the exchange of prisoners of war, and the following cartel was respectively signed and duly executed on the part of the two Governments. This important instrument of war invites a close examination of the reader, and is copied in full:

Haxall's Landing, on James River, July 22, 1862

The undersigned, having been commissioned by the authorities they respectively represent, to make arrangements for a general exchange of prisoners of war, have agreed to the following articles:

Article I.   It is hereby agreed and stipulated, that all prisoners of war held by either party, including those taken on private armed vessels, known as privateers, shall be exchanged upon the conditions and terms following:

Prisoners to be exchanged, man for man and officer for officer; privateers to be placed upon the footing of officers and men of the navy.

Men and officers of lower grades, may be exchanged for officers of a higher grade, and men and officers of different services may be exchanged according to the following scale of equivalents.

A general-commanding-in-chief; or an admiral, shall be exchanged for officers of equal rank or for sixty privates or common seamen.

A flag officer or major-general shall be exchanged for officers of equal rank or for forty privates or common seamen.

A commodore, carrying a broad pennant, or a brigadier-general shall be exchanged for officers of equal rank or twenty privates or common seamen.

A captain in the navy or a colonel shall be exchanged for officers of equal rank or for fifteen privates or common seamen.

A lieutenant-colonel, or commander in the navy, shall be exchanged for officers of equal rank or for ten privates or common seamen.

A lieutenant-commander or a major shall be exchanged for officers of equal rank or eight privates or common seamen.

A lieutenant or a master in the navy or a captain in the army or marines shall be exchanged for officers of equal rank or six privates or common seamen.

Master's mates in the navy, or lieutenants or ensigns in the army, shall be exchanged for officers of equal rank or four privates or common seamen.

Midshipmen, warrant officers in the navy, masters of merchant vessels and commanders of privateers, shall be exchanged for officers of equal rank or three privates or common seamen; second captains, lieutenants or mates of merchant vessels or privateers, and all petty officers in the navy, and all non-commissioned officers in the army or marines, shall be severally exchanged for persons of equal rank or for two privates or common seamen; and private soldiers or common seamen, shall be exchanged for each other, man for man.

Article II.   Local, State, civil, and militia rank held by persons not in actual military service, will not be recognized; the basis of exchange being the grade actually held in the naval and military service of the respective parties.

Article III.   If citizens held by either party on charges of disloyalty for any alleged civil offence are exchanged, it shall only be for citizens. Captured sutlers, teamsters, and all civilians in the actual service of either party to be exchanged for persons in similar position.

Article IV.   All prisoners of war to be discharged on parole in ten days after their capture, and the prisoners now held and those hereafter taken to be transported to the points mutually agreed upon, at the expense of the capturing party. The surplus prisoners, not exchanged, shall not be permitted to take up arms again, nor to serve as military police, or constabulary force in any fort, garrison, or field work, held by either of the respective parties, nor as guards of prisoners, deposit, or stores, nor to discharge any duty usually performed by soldiers, until exchanged under the provisions of this cartel. The exchange is not to be considered complete until the officer or soldier exchanged for has been actually restored to the lines to which he belongs.

Article V.   Each party, upon the discharge of prisoners of the other party, is authorized to discharge an equal number of their own officers or men from parole, furnishing at the same time to the other party a list of their prisoners discharged, and of their own officers and men relieved from parole; thus enabling each party to relieve from parole such of their own officers and men as the party may choose. The lists thus mutually furnished will keep both parties advised of the true condition of the exchange of prisoners.

Article VI.   The stipulations and provisions above mentioned to be of binding obligation during the continuance of the war, it matters not which party may have the surplus of prisoners, the great principles involved being: 1st. An equitable exchange of prisoners, man for man, officer for officer, or officers of higher grade, exchanged for officers of lower grade, or for privates, according to the scale of equivalents. 2d. That privates and officers and men of different services may be exchanged according to the same scale of equivalents. 3d. That all prisoners, of whatever arm of service, are to be exchanged or paroled in ten days from the time of their capture, if it be practicable to transfer them to their own lines in that time; if not, as soon thereafter as practicable. 4th. That no officer, soldier, employee in service of either party is to be considered as exchanged and absolved from his parole until his equivalent has actually reached the lines of his friends. 5th. That the parole forbids the performance of field, garrison, police, or guard, or constabulary duty.

JOHN A. DIX, *Major-General.*
D. H. HILL, *Major-General,*
C.S.A.

SUPPLEMENTARY ARTICLES.

Article VII.   All prisoners of war now held on either side, and all prisoners hereafter taken, shall be sent, with all reasonable despatch, to A. M. Aiken's, below Dutch Gap, on the James River, in Virginia, or to Vicksburg, on the Mississippi River, in the State of Mississippi, and there exchanged or paroled until such exchange can be effected, notice being previously given by each party of the number of prisoners it will send and the time when they will be delivered at those points respectively; and in case the vicissitudes of war shall change the military relations of the places designated in this article to the contending parties, so as to render the same inconvenient for the delivery and exchange of prisoners, other places, bearing as nearly as may be the present local relations of said places to the lines of said parties, shall be, by mutual agreement, substituted. But nothing in this article contained shall prevent the commanders of two opposing armies from exchanging prisoners, or releasing them on parole, at other points mutually agreed on by said commanders.

Article VIII. For the purpose of carrying into effect the foregoing articles of agreement, each party will appoint two agents, to be called agents for the exchange of prisoners of war, whose duty it shall be to communicate with each other, by correspondence and otherwise; to prepare the lists of prisoners; to attend to the delivery of the prisoners at the places agreed on, and to carry out promptly, effectually, and in good faith, all the details and provisions of the said articles of agreement.

Article IX. And in case any misunderstanding shall arise in regard to any clause or stipulation in the foregoing articles, it is mutually agreed that such misunderstanding shall not interrupt the release of prisoners on parole, as herein provided, but shall be made the subject of friendly explanation, in order that the object of this agreement may neither be defeated nor postponed.

JOHN A. DIX, *Major-General.*
D. H. HILL, *Major-General, C.S.A.*

Mr. Robert Ould was appointed agent of the Confederacy under this important text of the war. He was eminently qualified for the office. He was among the most accomplished jurists of the country; he had one of the most vigorous intellects in the Confederacy; He was a man of large humanity, dignified, and even lofty manners, and spotless personal honour. The record of his services in the cause of humanity and truth was one of the purest in either the public bureau or secret chamber of the Confederacy.

It will be seen that the chief, if not the only purpose, of the instrument copied above was to secure the release of all prisoners of war. To that end the fourth article provided that all prisoners of war should be discharged on parole in ten days after their capture, and that the prisoners then held and those thereafter taken should be transported to the points mutually agreed upon, at the expense of the capturing party. The sixth article also stipulated that "all prisoners of whatever arm of service are to be exchanged or paroled in ten days from the time of their capture, if it be practicable to transfer them to their own lines in that time; if not, as soon thereafter as practicable."

From the date of the cartel until July, 1863, the Confederate authorities held the excess of prisoners. During that interval deliveries were made as fast as the Federal Government furnished transportation. Indeed, upon more than one occasion, Commissioner Ould urged the Federal authorities to send increased means of transportation. As ready as the enemy always has been to bring false accusations against the Confederates, it has never been alleged that they failed or neglected to make prompt deliveries of prisoners who were not under charges when they held the excess. On the other hand, during the same time the cartel was openly and notoriously violated by the Federal authorities. Officers and men were kept in cruel confinement, sometimes in irons or doomed to cells, without charge or trial.

These facts were distinctly charged in the correspondence of Commissioner Ould. On the 26th July, 1863, he addressed a letter to Lieut.-Col. Ludlow, then acting as agent of exchange on the Federal side, in which he used the following impressive and vigorous language in vindication of himself and his Government: "Now that our official connection is being terminated, I say to you in the fear of God—and I appeal to Him for the truth of the declaration—that there has been no single moment, from the time we were first brought together in connection with the matter of exchange to the present hour, during which there has not been an open and notorious violation of the cartel, by your authorities. Officers and men, numbering over hundreds, have been, during your whole connection with the cartel, kept in cruel confinement, sometimes in irons, or doomed to cells, without charges or trial. They are in prison now, unless God, in His mercy, has released them. In our parting moments, let me do you the justice to say that I do not believe it is so much your fault as that of your authorities. Nay, more, I believe your removal from your position has been owing to the personal efforts you have made for a faithful observance, not only of the cartel, but of humanity, in the conduct of the war.

"Again and again have I importuned you to tell me of one officer or man now held in confinement by us, who was declared exchanged. You have, to those appeals, furnished one, Spencer Kellog. For him I have searched in vain. On the other hand, I appeal to your own records for the cases where your reports have shown that our officers and men have been held for long months and even years in violation of the cartel and our agreements. The last phase of the enormity, however, exceeds all others. Although you have many thousands of our soldiers now in confinement in your prisons, and especially in that horrible hold of death Fort Delaware, you have not, for several weeks, sent us any prisoners. During those weeks you have despatched Capt. Mulford with the steamer New York to City Point, three or four times, without any prisoners. For the first two or three times some sort of an excuse was attempted. None is given at this present arrival. I do not mean to be offensive when I say that effrontery could not give one. I ask you with no purpose of disrespect, what can you think of this covert attempt to secure the delivery of all your prisoners in our hands, without the release of those of ours who are languishing in hopeless misery in your prisons and dungeons?"

It is a fact beyond all controversy that officers and soldiers of the Confederacy entitled to delivery and exchange, were kept in confinement, in defiance of the cartel, some under charges, and some without. Many of these officers and soldiers were in confinement at the time of the adoption of the cartel, and continued to be so kept for months and years afterwards.

In a few instances Commissioner Ould succeeded by persistent pressure in securing their release. In other cases, when from returned prisoners he would learn their place of confinement, and state it to the Federal agent, there would either be a denial of the fact that the party was confined there, or he would be removed to some other prison. Many of these prisoners were actually declared exchanged by the Federal Agent of Exchange, but yet still kept in prison, and all the others were entitled to delivery for exchange under the terms of the cartel.

To the serious allegation of a retention of prisoners in spite of the cartel and all the obligations of good faith, the Federal Government never attempted anything but a paltry counter-charge of the weakest and most disingenuous kind. During the period before mentioned the only coin plaints made by the Federal authorities of any breach of the cartel, were in the cases of such officers as were retained in consequence of President Davis' several proclamations, and in the case of Gen. Streight and his officers. In looking back over the prison records of the Confederacy, the author can find no instance of any officers or men who were kept in prison after the date of the cartel under the proclamations of Mr. Davis. In point of fact, nothing was ever done under them. No inquiry was ever made whether the prisoners led negro troops or not. Streight's men were detained for several months. The reasons for their detention were fully given, In a letter written by Commissioner Ould, August 1st, 1863, to Brig.-Gen. Meredith, he said: "In retaining Col. Streight and his command, the Confederate authorities have not gone as far as those of the United States have claimed for themselves the right to go ever since the establishment of the cartel. You have claimed and exercised the right to retain officers and men indefinitely, not only upon charges actually preferred, but upon mere suspicion. You have now in custody officers who were in confinement when the cartel was framed, and who have since been declared exchanged. Some of them have been tried, but most of them have languished in prison all the weary time without trial or charges. I stand prepared to prove these assertions. This course was pursued, too, in the face not only of notice, but of protest. Do you deny to us the right to detain officers and men for trial upon grave charges, while you claim the right to keep in confinement any who may be the object of your suspicion or special enmity?"

Commissioner Ould also informed the Federal authorities, in 1863, that the charges against Streight and his command were not sustained, and that they were held as other prisoners. At the time, however, of this latter notification, other difficulties had supervened, which had almost entirely stopped exchanges.

Up to July, 1863, the Confederates had a large excess of prisoners. The larger number had been released upon parole after capture. Such paroles had been without question respected by both parties, until about the middle of 1863, when they were to be declared to be void (except under very special circumstances) by General Orders at Washington. The true reason of those General Orders was that the Federals had no lists of paroled prisoners (released on capture) to be charged against the Confederates. The latter had paid off all debts of that kind from their abundant stores. They, on the other hand, had many such lists which were unsatisfied, being principally captures in Kentucky, Tennessee, etc. Such being the state of affairs, on the 8th of April, 1863, Commissioner Ould was informed that "exchanges will be confined to such equivalents as are held in confinement on either side." In other words, as all the paroles held by the Federals had been satisfied and paid for in equivalents, and as they then held none of such to be charged against the Confederates, they would no longer respect such as they held, and the latter must deliver men actually in captivity for such as they would send. The Confederates then had the outstanding paroles, but the Federals had the majority of prisoners in hand. The effect of all this would have been, after the Confederates had delivered all their prisoners, to leave a large balance of their people in prison, while they at the same time had in their possession the paroles of ten times as many prisoners as the enemy held in captivity. This arrangement Commissioner Ould refused with indignation. The officers and men, who gave the paroles referred to, were subsequently, in violation of their parole, and without being declared exchanged, ordered to duty, and served against the South. Thereupon, Commissioner Ould off-setted such paroles against similar paroles taken by our officers and men at Vicksburg, and declared a like number of the latter exchanged. That was the only way he had of "getting even" with the enemy; and no one can say that the way was not fair and honourable.

From this time the provision of the cartel, that all prisoners, where practicable, were to be delivered within ten days was practically nullified, and was not respected during the remainder of the war. Such deliveries as were made afterwards, were in consequence of special agreements. The most strenuous efforts were made by Commissioner Ould to remedy this distressing state of things. The Confederate authorities only claimed that the provisions of the cartel should be fulfilled. They only asked the enemy to do what, without any hesitation, they had done during the first year of the operation of the cartel. Seeing a persistent purpose on the part of the Federal Government to violate its own agreement, the Confederate authorities, *moved by the sufferings of the men in the prisons of each belligerent,* determined to abate their fair demands, and accordingly, on the 10th of August, 1864, Commissioner Ould addressed the following communication to Major John E. Mulford, Assistant Agent of Exchange:

Richmond, VA
August 10, 1864

Maj. John E. Mulford, Asst. Agent of Exchange:

Sir: You have several times proposed to me to exchange the prisoners respectively held by the two belligerents, officer for officer, and man for man. The same offer has also been made by other officials having charge of matters connected with the exchange of prisoners. This proposal has heretofore been declined by the Confederate authorities, they insisting upon the terms of the cartel, which required the delivery of the excess on either side upon parole. In view, however, of the very large number of prisoners now held by each party, and the suffering consequent upon their continued confinement, I now consent to the above proposal and agree to deliver to you the prisoners held in captivity by the Confederate authorities, provided you agree to deliver an equal number of Confederate officers and men. As equal numbers are delivered from time to time, they will be declared exchanged. This proposal is made with the understanding that the officers and men on both sides, who have been longest in captivity, will be first delivered, where it is practicable. I shall be happy to hear from you as speedily as possible, whether this arrangement can be carried out.

Respectfully, your obedient servant,
R. OULD, *Agent of Exchange.*

The delivery of this letter was accompanied with a statement of the mortality which was hurrying so many Federal prisoners, at Andersonville to the grave.

On the 20th of the same month Major Mulford returned with the flag of truce steamer, but brought no answer to the letter of the 10th of August. In conversation with him, Commissioner Ould asked if he had any reply to make to the communication, and his answer was that he was not authorized to make any. So deep was the solicitude which Commissioner Ould felt in the fate of the captives in Northern prisons, that he determined to make another effort. In order to obviate any objection which technicality might raise as to the person to whom his communication was addressed, he wrote to Maj.-Gen. E. A. Hitchcock, the Federal Commissioner of Exchange, residing in Washington city, the following letter, and delivered the same to Major Mulford on the day of its date. Accompanying that letter was a copy of the communication which he had addressed to Major Mulford on the 10th of August:

Richmond, August 22, 1864.

Maj.-Gen. E. A. Hitchcock, U. S. Commissioner of Exchange:

Sir: Enclosed is a copy of a communication which, on the 10th inst., I addressed and delivered to Major Jno. E. Mulford, Assistant Agent of Exchange. Under the circumstances of the case, I deem it proper to forward this paper to you, in order that you may fully understand the position which is taken by the Confederate authorities. I shall be glad if the proposition therein made is accepted by your Government.

Respectfully your obedient servant
Ro. OULD, *Agent of Exchange.*

On the afternoon of the 30th August, Commissioner Ould was notified that the flag of truce steamer had again appeared at Varina. On the following day he sent to Maj. Mulford the following note

Richmond, August 31, 1864

Maj. John E. Mulford, Assistant Agent of Exchange:

Sir: On the 10th of this month I addressed you a communication, to which I have received no answer. On the 22d inst. I also addressed a communication to Maj.-Gen. E. A. Hitchcock, U. S. Commissioner of Exchange, enclosing a copy of my letter to you of the 10th inst. I now respectfully ask you to state in writing whether you have any reply to either of said communications; and if not, whether you have any reason to give why no reply has been made?

Respectfully, your obedient servant,
Ro. Ould, *Agent of Exchange*

In a short time Commissioner Ould received the following response:

Flag of Truce Steamer, "New York."
Varina, VA., August 31, 1864.

Hon. R. Ould, Agent of Exchange:

Sir: I have the honour to acknowledge the receipt of your favour of to-day, requesting answer, etc., to your communication of the 10th inst., on the question of the exchange of prisoners. To which, in reply, I would say, I have no communication on the subject from our authorities, nor am I yet authorized to make answer.

I am, sir, very respectfully,
Your obedient servant,
JOHN E. MULFORD, *Ass't Agent of Exchange.*

This was the whole Federal reply to the humane proposition of the Confederacy—this the brief indication of their cruel purpose to let their prisoners rot and die in insufficient prisons, merely for the purpose of pointing a libel and colouring a story against the Southern Confederacy. The offer of Commissioner Ould was on the extreme of generosity. He proposed, when the enemy had a large excess of prisoners, to exchange officer for officer and man for man. This arrangement would have left the surplus in the enemy's hands. But the liberal offer, which would have instantly restored to life and freedom thousands of suffering captives, was never even heeded at Washington; it was brutally calculated there that such a delivery from the prison pens of Andersonville and elsewhere would put so many thousand Confederate muskets in the field, and cut off a chapter of horrours, from which it had been convenient to draw texts on the subject of "rebel barbarities." To keep that text before the world was the determined purpose at Washington. It had again and again been announced that the subsistence of the Confederacy had fallen so low—chiefly through the warfare of the enemy making it a point to destroy in all parts of the country supplies of every kind—that its own soldiers were compelled to subsist upon a third of a pound of meat and a pound of coarse corn meal or flour every day. With such reduced rations, Confederate soldiers themselves were often exposed with thin and tattered clothes to the freezing winter storms, without tents, overcoats, blankets or shoes. In these circumstances it was impossible to provide properly for many tens of thousands of prisoners at Andersonville, Salisbury, and other places south of Richmond, where crowded quarters, prepared only for smaller numbers, and frequent removals to prevent recapture, added to the discomfort of the prisoners, and swelled the list of mortality. The authorities at Washington refused to do their own part to relieve the sufferings of these unhappy men, and deliberately decreed the extension of their sufferings that they might put before the world false and plausible proofs of "rebel barbarity."

It is simply in opposition to all that is known of Southern generosity in the war to believe that the sufferings of Andersonville were the result of neglect, still less of design on the part of the Confederate Government. A single train of acts is not likely to be so opposed to the whole career and consistent character of a people in a four years' war. The site of the prison at Andersonville-a point on the Southwestern railway in Georgia had been selected under an official order having reference to the following points: "A healthy locality, plenty of pure good water, a running stream, and, if possible, shade trees, and in the immediate neighbourhood of grist and saw mills." The pressure was so great at Richmond, and the supplies so scant, that prisoners were sent forward while the stockade was only about half finished. When the first instalment of prisoners arrived, there was no guard at Andersonville, and the little squad which had charge of them in the cars had to remain; and at no time did the guard, efficient and on duty, exceed fifteen hundred, to man the stockade, to guard, and do general duty, and afford relief and enforce discipline over thirty-four thousand prisoners.

In regard to the sufferings and mortality among the prisoners at Andersonville, none of it arose from the unhealthiness of the locality. The food, though the same as that used by the Confederate soldiers, the bread, too, being corn, was different from that to which they had been accustomed, did not agree with them, and scurvy and diarrhea prevailed to a considerable extent; neither disease, however, was the result of starvation. That some prisoners did not get their allowance, although a full supply was sent in, is true. But there not being a guard sufficient to attend to distribution, Federal prisoners were appointed, each having a certain number allotted to his charge, among whom it was his duty to see that every man got his portion, and, as an inducement, this prisoner had especial favours and advantages; upon complaint by those under him, he was broke and another selected; so that it only required good faith on the part of these head men, thus appointed, to insure to each man his share. But prisoners would often sell their rations for whiskey and tobacco, and would sell the clothes from their backs for either of them.

In regard to sanitary regulations, there were certain prescribed places and modes for the reception of all filth, and a sluice was made to carry it off; but the most abominable disregard was manifested of all sanitary regulations, and to such a degree that if a conspiracy had been entered into by a large number of the prisoners to cause the utmost filth and stench, it could not have accomplished a more disgusting result. Besides which there was a large number of atrocious villains, whose outrages in robbing, beating and murdering their fellow-prisoners must have been the cause, directly or remotely, of very many deaths and of an inconceivable amount of suffering. We must recollect that among thirty-four thousand prisoners, who had encountered the hardships of the fields of many battles, and had had wounds, there were many of delicate physique—many of respectability, to whom such fellowship, such self-created filth, and such atrocious ruffianism, would of itself cause despondency, disease, and death; and when, in addition to this, was the conviction that the Federal War Department, perfectly cognizant of all this, had deliberately consigned them indefinitely to this condition, a consuming despair was superadded to all their other sufferings.

The merits of Andersonville may be summed up by saying that it was of unquestioned healthfulness; it was large enough and had water enough, and could have been made tolerable for the number originally intended for it. It appears that the increase of that number was apparently a matter of necessity for the time; that other sites were selected and prepared with all possible despatch; that the provisions were similar in amount and quality to those used by Confederate soldiers; that deficient means rendered a supply of clothing, tents, and medicines scanty; that the rules of discipline and sanitary regulations of the prison, *if complied with by the prisoners,* would have secured to each a supply of food, and have averted almost, if not altogether, the filth and the ruffianism, which two causes outside of unavoidable sickness, caused the great mass of suffering and mortality.

View looking southward. Wartime photo by
Georgia photographer A. J. Riddle.
Courtesy of the National Park Service.

But the history of the extraordinary efforts of the Confederate authorities to relieve the sufferings of Andersonville, through some resumption of exchanges, does not end with the proposition referred to as made by Commissioner Ould to exchange man for man, and leave the surplus at the disposition of the enemy. It was followed by another more liberal and more extraordinary proposition. Acting under the direct instructions of the Secretary of War, and seeing plainly that there was no hope of any general or extended partial system of exchange, Commissioner Ould, in August, 1864, offered to the Federal agent of exchange, Gen. Mulford, to deliver to him all the sick and wounded Federal prisoners we had, *without insisting upon the delivery of an equivalent number of our prisoners in return.* He also informed Gen. Mulford of the terrible mortality among the Federal prisoners, urging him to be swift in sending transportation to the mouth of the Savannah River for the purpose of taking them away. The offer of Commissioner Ould included all the sick and wounded at Andersonville and other Confederate prisons. He further informed Gen. Mulford, in order to make his Government safe in sending transportation, that if the sick and wounded did not amount to ten or fifteen thousand men, the Confederate authorities would make up that number in well men. This offer, it will be recollected, was made early in August, 1864. Gen. Mulford informed Commissioner Ould it was directly communicated to his Government, yet no timely advantage was ever taken of it.

This interesting and important fact is for the first time authoritatively published in these pages. It contains volumes of significance. The question occurs, who was responsible for the sufferings of the sick and wounded and prisoners at Andersonville, from August to December, 1864? The world will ask with amazement, if it was possible that thousands of prisoners were left to die in inadequate places of confinement, merely to make a case against the South—merely for romance! The single fact gives the clue to the whole story of the deception and inhuman cruelty of the authorities at Washington with reference to their prisoners of war—the key to a chapter of horrours that even the hardy hand of History shakes to unlock. To blacken the reputation of an honourable enemy; to make a false appeal to the sensibilities of the world; to gratify an inhuman revenge, Mr. Stanton, the saturnine and malignant Secretary of War at Washington, did not hesitate to doom to death thousands of his countrymen, and then to smear their sentinels with accusing blood.

It was the purpose of Commissioner Ould to keep open the offer he had made, and deliver to the Federal authorities all their sick and wounded, from time to time, especially if the straits of war should deny the Confederates the means of providing for their comfort. To show how honest and earnest he was in his offer to Mulford, when the transportation did arrive, he did deliver to him at Savannah and Charleston thirteen thousand men, large numbers of whom were well, and was ready to deliver as many as his transportation could accommodate, and that too under the difficulties and pressure of Sherman's invasion of Georgia, when nothing but temporary shiftings were our expedients.

The transfer of the entire matter of the exchange of prisoners from the control of Secretary Stanton, who had been averse to all arguments of justice, and to all appeals on this subject, to that of Gen. Grant, offered to Commissioner Ould another opportunity to essay an effort of humanity. On the 11th February, 1865, he proposed to Gen. Grant, to deliver without delay all the prisoners on hand, upon receiving an assurance from him that he would deliver an equal number of Confederate prisoners, within a reasonable time. This was accepted, and every energy was used to send immediately through Wilmington, James River, and other practicable ways, all the prisoners we had. This was very speedily consummated, so far as all in prisons in Virginia, and North and South Carolina, were concerned. The presence of the enemy, and the cutting of our communications, only prevented the immediate execution elsewhere. Orders to that effect, and messengers to secure it, were sent to Georgia, Alabama, and the Trans-Mississippi. A return number of prisoners, to the amount of about five thousand per week, were sent to Richmond, until the fortunes of war closed all operations, even down to the matter of an adjustment of accounts. The adjustment has never been made.

James Madison Page

Chapter Three

The Dead Line and How the Raiders Were Executed (1908)

James Madison Page, a second lieutenant in Company A of the Sixth Michigan Cavalry, was "discovered and made a prisoner by the Fifth Virginia Cavalry" in the Eastern theatre of the war. Page's wartime odyssey included imprisonment at Belle Island and Andersonville. In 1908, Page felt compelled to write *The True Story of Andersonville Prison* subtitled *A Defense of Major Wirz* in order to counter harsh criticisms being leveled by other Union Prisoners. This book, published by the Neale Company of New York and Washington, is not as widely distributed as others penned by former prisoners, probably because Page provides a viewpoint similar to Southerners of the time. This book is available in reprint from the Iberian Publishing Company, 548 Cedar Creek Drive, Athens, Georgia 30605-3408.

I think that it was about the first of May that a lieutenant with a squad of negroes began to put up a railing fifteen feet from the stockade. If I am not mistaken the lieutenant's name was Davis. They took boards about six inches wide, such as are used in fence building, and set posts into the ground every fifteen feet and nailed the boards on top of the posts. This was known as the "dead-line." I was absent when, in the course of their building, they reached our quarters, and when I returned I found my comrades very much distressed and alarmed. They told me the lieutenant and his men were there; that the officer measured the ground from the palisade and they had found that our house was three feet within the prescribed limit of the dead-line; that it was but twelve feet from the stockade, and that the officer ordered them to move it at once. This was indeed a calamity.

We were discussing the matter when the young officer appeared on the scene. We called his attention to the crowded condition of the ground about us. It was the most desirable part of the camp and in our immediate vicinity there was not a square foot of unoccupied ground.

"I cannot help it," said he; "I am carrying out my orders, and if you cannot move the cabin you will have to take it down."

There was no use expostulating with him. He left, giving us an hour, I think it was, to move our habitation. We were speechless. He returned at the specified time, flew in a rage to find that we had done nothing, and used some very strong English.

"If you care to retain your building material," exclaimed the irate officer, "you had better get it away from here in the next twenty minutes. I will give you that time." He looked at his watch with the declaration that he would return in twenty minutes, and if the building was not moved that he would confiscate the whole thing.

Some of the boys suggested taking the house down and cutting off a few feet of the logs and rebuilding it inside of the dead-line; but this plan was not feasible and I told them that I would try to see Captain Wirz at once, and in case the Lieutenant returned before I did to explain matters to him, and try stay his hand.

The boys were dismayed at the situation, and doubted their ability to do anything with the officer in the mean time, and doubted still more that the Captain would help us.

I made as good time as a sick man could to the south gate, and fortunately I saw Wirz just entering it. I saluted and said, "Captain, we are in serious trouble at our quarters, and we want you to help us out. I hate to bother you but you are our only refuge now." "What is the trouble?" "Before the stockade was completed a sergeant in Colonel Person's regiment stationed here directed us while building our cabin to be sure and not build it closer to the stockade than twelve feet. We followed his instructions, and to make sure of it the end nearest to the wall is twelve feet from it. Now the lieutenant building the dead-line has ordered us to move it or take it down. The space adjacent to the cabin is so densely crowded that it is impossible to move it intact, and we cannot take it down as we do not know where to locate it." "Can you not shorten it in some way?" I explained why that could not be done. "Where are you located?" "Almost directly under sentry box number 35." "Very well, I'll go up with you and see for myself." He walked with me to our quarters, two hundred and fifty yards southeast of the gate.

When we came in sight of our house I saw that it was still there and the boys were all outside, the most of them sitting on the "piazza." They arose as we approached, and I could see surprise on their countenances. Wirz looked the situation over carefully while we were narrowly eyeing him, and I caught the faintest glimmer of a smile on his face as he said, pointing with his hand to the extreme southerly end of the cabin, "Who sleeps there?" "That is where I sleep, Captain," said I. "Well," said he, "you must be careful and not get up inside the dead-line." Then he went on, looking at all of us, "Men, let your quarters stand, and when Lieutenant Davis returns tell him that such are my orders, and not to interfere with your cabin. He can make a short offset in his line and go by without much trouble."

We heartily thanked him, and Billy Bowles was very enthusiastic over the outcome of the affair, and yelled, "Hurrah for Captain Wirz!" and we and some of our neighbors heartily joined in the cheering.

The cabin stood where it was originally built. It was not moved or taken down. This fact will be remembered by many ex-prisoners who are now living, as this incident was often referred to and discussed at the prison. We had the distinction of occupying the only house, cabin, hut, quarters, or habitation within the dead-line at Andersonville!

There was no question about the dead-line itself. It was, during the summer of 1864 at Andersonville, a stubborn fact. The railing was a well-defined sign of demarcation. It was the visible warning of "thus far and no farther," and every prisoner within the inclosure knew it. They well knew that to get within that proscribed space meant death at the hands of the sentries, and there were prisoners killed by the guards inside the dead-line at Andersonville. This was wrong.

It was cruel. It was also cruel to shoot prisoners within the inclosures of Point Pleasant and Johnson's Island, where they were confined. In this peaceful time, to the casual observer, the shooting down of poor, often sick, helpless prisoners of war inside an inclosure must seem the very height of barbarity. Nevertheless, it was done at every prison in the North and in the South. We have been for forty years denouncing the South without discovering "the beam in our own eye." It is a clear case of those "living in glass houses." But we have been imitating Aesop's wolf at the stream. As Sherman says, War is hell."

I have read articles written by commandants of Northern prisons setting forth the fact that the rebels killed were not fired at until the sentries had first ordered them to halt or fall back. I believe this to be the absolute truth.

On the other hand, while there were Union prisoners deliberately shot down during the daytime inside the dead-line at Andersonville, or "Camp Sumter," as the rebels called it, I believe that the sentries, before firing, ordered them back. That was my understanding of the matter, as it was also the understanding of the other prisoners. We understood that the order, "Prisoner, halt; get back beyond the line!" or a similar command must precede the act of firing.

There were well defined "neighborhoods" at Andersonville, and one day in the latter part of July a prisoner in our "neighborhood" was killed by a sentry. I am not sure whether it was the sentry at post 34 or 36; but at any rate, the rumor had it that the sentry fired without a word of warning and killed the unfortunate prisoner. The charge was contradicted by others living near the sentry box. It was also stated that the poor prisoner was partially deaf and did not hear the warning, and from his intense suffering he had become somewhat demented. At any rate, he was killed. I talked with Captain Wirz about the affair and from what he said I was satisfied that his orders to the guards were not to fire unless the prisoner failed to halt or return beyond the line. Said he, "I will investigate this matter." The sentry who had done the shooting was not seen at the post afterward.

Some of our writers boldly assert that no command to halt or warning was given before the shooting; that sentries were keenly on the alert to find a prisoner inside the line to fire on him, because for every prisoner killed within the dead- line the sentry was entitled to a thirty days' furlough. These same writers claim that prisoners with a leg or arm within the dreaded inclosure, and even the prisoner who would inadvertently place his hand on the railing, was killed. This is a monstrous charge!

One of those Andersonville writers, the loudest in maintaining that no warning was given by the sentries, rather stumbles in his statements, for he relates a case of a deaf prisoner who "did not hear the command to halt" and "was ruthlessly shot down."

The report of the "thirty days' furlough" for the sentry who shot a man within the dead-line was rife at Andersonville, but it was the easiest thing imaginable to start a rumor. No statement, no matter how weird, wonderful, improbable, wild or incredible, once started in the prison, would fail to have its couriers, its relators, and its believers.

We had a small-pox scare among the prisoners quite early in the history of the prison. There were a few sick within the inclosure who were brought down by the terrible malady. These persons were hurriedly and promptly taken from us and isolated; a commendable act upon the part of Captain Wirz and the medical men.

Contemporary view of stockade grounds
with "Dead-line" identified by markers.

There was an order for prompt and immediate vaccination, but the prisoners who could show that they had been treated shortly before were not interfered with. Others were vaccinated with fatal results in many cases. Many of those were compelled to go to the hospital, whereupon some garrulous individual started the fire that has never been quenched, viz. that there was poison in the vaccine matter. The truth is, the poison was in the impoverished blood of the patient, which could not grapple with varioloid, and not in the vaccine matter.

The so-called "dead-line" was a thing maintained in prisons, both North and South, during the Civil War. The line itself was a reality, there was no guess-work about it. To pass beyond it and to refuse or fail to halt or turn back when ordered by the sentry meant death, or at the very least a severe wound. The prisoner knew that he was taking his life in his hands when he crossed the dead-line and ignored the commands of the sentry.

I do not propose to argue as to whether it was right or wrong; that it was cruel admits of no denial, but it appears to be recognized by the rules of war.

According to the rules of war the soldier deserting "in the face of the enemy" merits death, and the soldier striking his superior officer and one who knowingly and willfully disobeys the orders of his superior officer, upon conviction by court-martial, cannot expect less.

I have now given my opinion of the dead-line, humble and inconsequential though it may be; at all events, authorities, both North and South, considered this war measure necessary.

The guards at all the prisons were but few in comparison to the number of prisoners. It is true that the guards were armed, but they could have been overpowered with little difficulty had there not been strict discipline and certain restrictions placed upon the prisoners. At the time that there were more than 30,000 prisoners at Andersonville I do not think the guards numbered over 800.

A great deal has been said by other writers about the hundreds upon hundreds of prisoners killed within the dead-line, but I say right here that the number was few, and I deny the further assertion that some were killed who only had one foot accidentally outside the line or unintentionally laid their hands upon the railing which marked the dead-line. So far as my knowledge of Andersonville goes, the statement is untrue.

John McElroy, who wrote "A Story of Rebel Prisons," and who was a prisoner at Andersonville, and, with the exception of Mr. Spencer, the most bitter and unfair against Captain Wirz and the rebels, says (pp. 156 157):

> "The only man I ever knew to be killed by the Twenty-sixth Alabama (the regiment guarding Andersonville) was named Hubbard, from Chicago, and a member of the Thirtyeighth Illinois. He was continually hobbling about chattering in a loud, discordant voice, saying all manner of hateful and annoying things wherever he had an opportunity. This and his beak-like nose gained for him the name of 'Poll Parrot.' His misfortune caused him to be tolerated where another man would have been suppressed. By-and-by he gave still greater cause for offense by his obsequiousness to curry favor with Wirz, who took him outside several times for purposes that were not well explained. Finally, some hours after Poll Parrot's visits outside, a rebel officer came in with a guard and proceeded with suspicious directness to a tent which was the mouth of a large tunnel that a hundred men or more had been quietly pushing forward, broke the tunnel in, and took the occupants outside for punishment. The questions that demanded immediate solution then were, 'Who is the traitor? Who informed the rebels?'

> "Suspicion pointed very strongly to Poll Parrot. By the next morning the evidence collected seemed to amount to a certainty, and a crowd caught the Parrot with the intention of lynching him. He succeeded in breaking away from them, and ran under the dead-line near where I was sitting in my tent. At first it looked as if he had done this to secure the protection of the guard. The latter, a Twenty-sixth Alabamian, ordered him out. Poll Parrot arose, put his back against the dead-line faced the guard, and said in his harsh, cackling voice, 'No, I won't go out. I have lost the confidence of my comrades and I want to die.'

> "Part of the crowd were taken back by this move, and felt disposed to take it as a demonstration of the Parrot's innocence. The rest thought it was a piece of bravado be c a u s e of his belief that the rebels would not injure him after he had served them. They renewed their yells, the guard ordered the Parrot out again, but the latter, tearing open his blouse, cackled out, 'No, I won't go; fire at me, guard. There's my heart; shoot me right there.'

"There was no help for it, the sentry leveled his gun and fired. The charge struck the Parrot's lower jaw and carried it completely away, leaving his tongue and the roof of his mouth exposed. As he was carried back to die he wagged his tongue vigorously in attempting to speak, but it was of no use.

"The guard set his gun down and buried his face in his hands."

The above is a garbled account. Mr. McElroy states facts as far as he goes, but he doesn't go far enough.

In the first place, the shooting of Hubbard occurred at least two months after the Alabama regiment left Andersonville—the Twenty-fifth instead of the Twenty-sixth, as McElroy puts it. It was some time about the middle of June that this occurred. Hubbard had lost his right leg at Chickamauga and had come a prisoner to Andersonville as early as April. He was an inoffensive, garrulous creature, and on account of his almost helpless condition had received favors at the hands of Captain Wirz. This tunnel that Mr. McElroy described was in the immediate vicinity of our cabin and some of my friends were concerned in the work. It was not generally known at the time, but later on we ascertained the fact that the Confederate authorities had one of their men disguised as a prisoner among us as a night spy. We subsequently learned he was busy spying about of nights. Several tunnels were started in the prison, and it was a surprise to us how readily the guard could locate them.

Before our knowledge of this spy's presence and work among us suspicion pointed to this prisoner or that as the informer. Hence, poor Hubbard became the victim.

My personal acquaintance with Hubbard led me to believe him innocent. I walked by the side of Hubbard on his way to the south gate, where he was followed by the mob charging him with being a traitor and declaring that if he did not get out of the stockade they would kill him. I had great sympathy with the man, doubting then, as I do now, that he had any knowledge of the location of the tunnel. When he reached the small gate in the dead line at the main entrance he pushed through, disregarding the command of the sentinel to halt, and sat down on the ground four or five feet outside of the dead-line, out of reach of the mob. Here he sat with his crutches across his lap and rocked his body back and forth, bewailing his fate, and when ordered back by the sentinel, with the threat that if he did not go he would shoot, he bared his breast and told him to shoot, that he would rather be killed by him than by his own comrades.

The sentinel called for an officer, and Captain Wirz appeared from the outside. Upon learning the cause of the disturbance Captain Wirz talked to the excited prisoners for several minutes, assuring them that Hubbard was innocent; that he had frequently taken him outside for recreation and food, and urged them to withhold their wrath and let him come back into the prison. He turned to Hubbard and told him to go back inside, that the boys would not harm him, and then he withdrew. The guard ordered poor "Poll Parrot" out three times, and then shot him dead, the ball passing through his head and breaking his well leg.

The sentry performed this duty reluctantly. He was goaded to the act by the taunts of the prisoners seeking Hubbard's death, shouting to him, 'You are a tin soldier, a wooden soldier!" and such taunts because he delayed firing. When he had at length fired the fatal shot he set down his musket and buried his face in his hands.

The clamor and violence of our prisoners, the passion of a howling mob, drove a poor, heartbroken, one-legged fellow-prisoner to his death.

Thiers, in his "History of the French Revolution," says "a mob is insane." I believe it.

After Hubbard died those who had been the loudest crying for his death were the busiest explaining why and how they knew that he was innocent.

I never could understand why Captain Wirz was condemned and executed at Washington, on November 10, 1865, unless it was for the murder of poor "Poll Parrot."

Captain Wirz had no kindergarten to deal with. The very fact that we were reluctantly compelled to put six of our own fellow-prisoners to death in order to maintain discipline shows the difficulty the commandant had to grapple with.

I have carefully read Spencer's account of the court martial of Wirz, and the evidence and addresses of counsel for the prosecution and defense, and there is not one word of evidence introduced touching upon the fact that we ourselves executed six of our comrades; but no one will deny that this gang, possibly with one exception, richly deserved death.

Early in May it developed that the prison camp was infested with an organized band of thieves and cutthroats who committed their depredations upon sick and helpless prisoners. At first they confined their operations to the darkness of night, but, becoming emboldened, stronger in number and organization, they got so they did not hesitate to attack their fellow-prisoners in the daytime. The leaders of this band of "raiders," as we called them, were thieves, bounty-jumpers, "wharf-rats," and graduates generally from the schools of corruption in large cities.

This band was daily being augmented as the number of prisoners increased, and by the first of June it seemed from their activity and their audacity that more than half the able-bodied prisoners belonged to the dreaded gang, and as yet there was no organization to oppose them.

Robberies became common even in the daytime. Men were robbed of everything of value—money, watches, rings, blankets, clothing, and even of their scanty rations. The gang had the camp intimidated, and seemed to have such absolute control that the report went about the camp that Wirz was in league with them. This I never for a moment believed. A reign of terror existed. We were a large and growing community without a government.

By the earnest request of the leading prisoners in my neighborhood, on June 7 I sought and obtained an interview with Wirz. I explained the situation briefly and asked his advice and assistance. After considering a moment, he said, "I understand the condition and have been wondering what the outcome would be. I can see only one way now. If you men can organize a sufficient force to arrest those scoundrels, and bring them to the gates, letting me know when you begin operations, and when you are ready to turn them over, I will arrange to have guards to take charge of them. Then you can organize a court of some kind, get your witnesses and men to take charge of the prosecution and defense, and I will let you prisoners take charge of the whole matter. You can then come outside and try them. Now, if you prisoners conclude to undertake this, and you certainly ought to do something, keep me apprised of your progress and I will be only too glad to assist you as far as in my power. I will at once present the matter to General Winder."

As to whether or not I was the first prisoner to approach Captain Wirz relative to this matter, I do not know, but he acted as if the subject had not been broached to him before.

It was evident that Wirz gave this his prompt attention, by the following general order, which is a matter of record and speaks for itself:

"Camp Sumter, Andersonville, Ga.,
"June 30, 1864.

'General Orders No. 57.

"A gang of evil-disposed persons among the prisoners of war at this post having banded themselves together for the purpose of assaulting, murdering, and robbing their fellow-prisoners, and having already committed all of these deeds, it becomes necessary to adopt measures to protect the lives and property of the prisoners against the acts of these men, and in order that this may be accomplished, the well-disposed prisoners may, and they are hereby authorized to, establish a court among themselves for the trial and punishment of such offenders.

"On such trials the charges will be distinctly made with specifications setting forth time and place, a copy of which will be furnished the accused.

"The whole proceeding will be kept in writing, all the testimony will be fairly written out as nearly in the words of the witnesses as possible.

"The proceedings, findings, and sentence in each case will be sent to the commanding officer for record, and if found in order and proper, the sentence will be ordered for execution.

"By order of Brig. Gen. John H. Winder.

W. A. WINDER,
"Asst. *Adjutant General*

Not a solitary writer of the many stories of Andersonville that I have read since the war has been disposed to do justice to Captain Wirz, and they have done him a great injustice in this matter. So far as I know, the idea that brought about the overthrow of the murderous raiders came from Wirz himself; and it is certain that the efforts of "Limber Jim" (James Laughlin), Key, Corrigan, Larkin, Johnson, and others, of the "law and order" organization, and of the police force, all of whom deserve great credit in arresting the "raiders," would have been fruitless but for the cooperation of Wirz.

From this time on the great question was how to meet and break up the thieving organization, but no real action was taken until the last of June. It is my recollection that the police organization was perfected on July 1. The "raiders" were not idle. They knew of the character and scope of our work as soon as we began. On July 1 Captain Wirz was notified the work of arresting suspects would begin the following day, July 2.

During three days, July 2, 3 and 4, we arrested one hundred and seventy-five men and turned them over to the guards at the south gate. There were many witnesses, and the trial lasted six days, and resulted in the conviction of six on the charge of murder in the first degree. These men were sentenced to be hanged July 11. Their names were as follows: Charles Curtis, Company A, Fifth Rhode Island Infantry; Pat Delaney, Company E, Eighty-third Pennsylvania Volunteers; F. Sullivan, Seventy-second New York Volunteers; A. Muer, of the United States Navy; J. Sarsfield, One Hundred and Forty-fourth New York Volunteers, and Wm. Collins, Company D, Eighty-eighth Pennsylvania Infantry. Collins was known in the camp as "Mosby," having received the sobriquet from his daring and rushing proclivities. Had he exhibited the same spirit of dare-deviltry on the field of battle that he did in waylaying his fellow-prisoners it might have redounded to his military distinction.

Twenty-five of the convicted men were sentenced to wear ball and chain during their imprisonment.

One of the most startling developments to me in this trial was the conviction of Pat Delaney of murder. We had been neighbors in our prison life for many months, both at Belle Isle and at Andersonville. He was sent from Belle Isle with the same detachment that my comrades were. He was always ready to help others and appeared to take great pleasure in doing some kind act for my comrades and myself. He appeared always to have money and plenty to eat, and he was extremely generous with both. I was under many obligations to him, and I always regarded him as a brave, generous Irishman. A chapter could be written on the generous qualities of this unfortunate man. I sought to save him, but was confronted with overwhelming testimony of his guilt. To me it looked like a case of "poor dog Tray." It was agreed upon beforehand among the regulators that the guilty would have to take their medicine.

The court conducting the trial was regularly organized and officered, and the proceedings were regularly recorded, with the intention of making a full report later to the Government.

On the morning of the 11th a team loaded with materials for the gallows was sent in by Wirz, and our men, who were carpenters, erected the gallows in the street seventy-five yards east from the deadline at the south gate.

A solid mass of prisoners gathered about the place, and at two o'clock Wirz came in riding his gray horse, at the head of the six doomed men, who were heavily guarded. The condemned men, tied together, walked in double file, Delaney and Curtis in advance. At the foot of the platform the Captain gave the command "halt," and turning toward us he said, "Here, men, I return these prisoners to you in as good condition as I received them. I have carried out my part of the agreement, and now whatever you may do with these men I must remind you that the Confederate Government is in no way responsible. You will do with them as you please, and may God have mercy on you and them."

With all McElroy's prejudice against Wirz he cannot strip this speech of its evident fairness. His version of the incident, given in his story of Andersonville, is different, I know, but I was standing at this time within a few feet of the gallows.

After turning the culprits over to the police, Wirz and his guard withdrew, and I heard Curtis say, "Delaney, what do you propose to do about this? As for me, I am going to make a break." At this he slipped the cord from his wrist, and broke through the dense crowd of prisoners like a mad bull. His attempted escape created great excitement, and a shell or two went singing over the prison, I presume to remind us that our guards were ready for business and would allow no stampede toward the gate. Laughlin (Limber Jim), the sheriff or marshal of the day, despatched several of the police after Curtis, and the hangman led the other five up the steps onto the platform. They were placed on the trap under the cross-bar, from which were dangling six nooses. The condemned men were placed in position and each noose adjusted. Curtis was soon brought back and placed in position, and all was ready; but there was some delay, as each one of the condemned had some message to send to wife, mother, or friend. Some of them did not expect to die. I do not think that Delaney thought that the "regulators" would take extreme measures, for he smiled as the noose was placed around his neck. Laughlin ordered the caps (meal bags) to be drawn over their heads. The trap was sprung and five of them swung into eternity. The rope around Collins' neck broke and he fell to the ground, apparently unhurt. He rose to his feet and begged piteously for his life, but Laughlin laid his hand on his shoulder and said, "Collins, words are useless now. You are condemned to die and die you must." Then Collins regained his composure, mounted the steps with firmness, took his place beside the quivering, dangling bodies, and died without a word.

After Delaney was sentenced I had a talk with him. Said he, "Jim, I am innocent. I'll admit that I associated with the marauders; that I received money from them because I was hungry and starving. You know I had money, but I never assaulted a man nor stole a dollar; but here I am about to die. Ah, that is what comes of keeping bad company."

He sent for Father Hamilton, and that evening received extreme unction at the hands of the priest.

It was reported, but I did not know of it personally, that Father Hamilton begged for the life of Delaney.

Father Hamilton, a Southerner, was greatly beloved by the prisoners. He was kind to all of us, Catholic and Protestant alike. When we would ask him if there was any news of exchanging prisoners he would say, "Poor men, I have given my word not to communicate any information," and he would sadly shake his head and turn away.

Those marauders had even murdered fellow prisoners in quest of booty. This was proved beyond doubt at the trial by good and reliable eye-witnesses. More than one man lost his life by trying to defend himself and protect his property. The witnesses had by threats of intimidation kept silent, and moreover they "had troubles of their own" to occupy their minds.

During the "reign of terror" the gang was so powerful in numbers and strength of organization that it controlled things and operated with a high hand. It was a terrible state of affairs.

One morning shortly after daylight, while on my way to the creek to wash, I came across a prisoner, not more than three hundred feet from our quarters, lying on his back dead. He had his throat cut, evidently with a razor, as that was the weapon usually used by the raiders.

But the terrible uncontrolled dominion of the thug and murderer was at an end. We could breathe easier, and within the lines could go and come as we pleased day or night. Prior to the organization of the regulators we were constantly on the lookout, and dared not venture from our quarters after dark; for after dark the terrible marauder had full swing.

Those who were acquitted by the court were yet suspected guilty by the body of prisoners, and when they were turned back into the prison they were obliged to run the gauntlet between two lines of their fellow-prisoners, who showered upon them so many blows that three died from the injuries thus received. I took no hand in this business; it seemed to me the height of brutality. I had no doubt at the time that some of those punished were innocent, but, however cruel, the great majority of them richly deserved what they got. "Limber Jim" (or Laughlin) took a prominent part in punishing the offenders. His brother had been robbed and killed by the raiders.

The men that were tried and punished had hundreds of friends and sympathizers among the prisoners, and July 11, 12 and 13 things looked ominous in the stockade. Threats were openly made and prisoners were massing toward opposite sides.

It was thought best among the regulators to ask Captain Wirz to parole Sergeant Key, Corrigan, "Limber Jim," and the hangmen who officiated at the execution, as a precautionary measure. This was done. Had they remained among us they would doubtless have been killed.

On the morning of July 14 the dead body of a prisoner named Heffron was found near the south gate. He was a prominent witness against the raiders, and one who had testified in the daytime. Night sessions of the trial had been held and it was a favorite time for witnesses for the prosecution to put in an appearance.

For a few days the situation looked gloomy indeed. The reign of terror threatened to grow even more frightful.

During the summer months at Andersonville there was a feeling between the "Eastern" and "Western" soldiers which in some instances amounted almost to hatred. Key, Corrigan, Laughlin—"Limber Jim," and Larkin were from the West.

The raiders were now without a leader, and the hanging of six of their prominent members cowed them almost into submission; but had there been one of them possessed with a daring and audacity of Curtis or Collins on July 12 or 13 there would have been a battle in the prison in which no doubt many men would have been killed and wounded. It would have been a battle which the guards would have been powerless to suppress.

Meanwhile we were not idle, but kept up and added to our organization. In this we had the advantage of the raiders and their friends, for on the 12th and 13th they contented themselves with uttering threats and assaulting some of the regulators.

After Key left, Sergeant A. R. Hill, of the One Hundredth Ohio, was elected as our chief. He was a large, strong, and powerful man, twenty-eight or thirty years of age, and came into prominence at Belle Isle by "licking" Jack Oliver, the conceded champion among us.

Hill appointed several hundred policemen, who had secret passwords, and signal whistles to summon help. For the first few days of the Hill administration there was much disturbance and several fights, but the victory was on the side of the regulators, and in a few days quiet and order reigned.

The marauders were subdued, a number were punished, and "raiding" was at an end.

After Wirz, those entitled particularly to the credit of bringing about order and tranquilizing affairs were Sergeant Key, of an Illinois regiment; Laughlin, Larkin, Corrigan, Johnson, and others whose names I do not recall.

My reason for going into this matter to considerable length is that the other writers have treated the affair so meagerly and have withheld the credit due to Wirz.

I have at hand five histories of Andersonville. Some of the writers dismiss the subject with a paragraph. None, except McElroy, gives the names of the men hanged. None, except Kellogg and Urban, gives any credit to Wirz, if credit it can be called. Both state the same thing, and I quote from Urban's "Battlefield and Prison Pen" (pp. 326, 327):

> "Robert H. Kellogg, sergeant-major of the Sixteenth Connecticut Volunteers, who was in Andersonville at the time, and who is the author of an interesting work called 'Life and Death in Rebel Prisons,' writes of that affair in the following words [speaking of prisoners daily coming in plentifully supplied with money, jewelry, etc.]: 'These newcomers afforded the raiders, or camp robbers, fresh opportunities to continue their work. They seized upon one of these and it soon proved to be a robbery in earnest. After severely beating and cutting his head they took his watch and $175 in money. He entered a complaint to Captain Wirz, and the whole camp being completely aroused, collected around with clubs and began to arrest the gang as fast as possible."

I refrain from further quotation, except to prove "out of their own mouths" that their histories are misleading.

Urban says again (pp. 330, 331):

> "Hid in the ground where the villains stayed were found watches, money, and different kinds of weapons; also the body of a man the miscreants had put out of the way."

That statement is all right, but the following statement is all wrong (p. 331):

> "The valuables were taken possession of by the rebels, who no doubt rejoiced at the proceedings, as it not only enriched themselves but also weakened their enemies."

Every article, so far as I know, that was identified by a prisoner at the trial, was turned over to the owner.

Certain authors like Richardson and Kellogg allege that a most scrutinizing and careful search was made at all the rebel prisons, and that every article, valuable or otherwise, was taken from prisoners and never returned; that it was robbery on the part of rebel officers and guards.

Now for a little circumstantial or presumptive evidence to the contrary.

The marauders—our fellow-prisoner at Andersonville robbed their fellow-prisoners of thousands of dollars, and also more than a score of watches, besides jewelry of various kinds and descriptions.

How about, "After it was known that there were thieves operating, men took off their watchchains and watch-cords on account of the industry of the pick-pockets."

Hanging of the raiders by Union prisoners.
Courtesy of the National Park Service.

Were the rebel officers and guards unable to see watch-chains and watch-cords?

Let us hear the evidence of Mr. Ambrose Spencer in his book, "A Narrative of Andersonville" (p. 72):

> "As each train arrived squads of ten men were taken into a detached building nearby, where Wirz, R. B. Winder, and W. S. Winder were assembled. There each man was searched by Duncan and Humes, was stripped to his shirt, if he possessed one, his shoes were closely scrutinized and the soles examined, and the shoes themselves appropriated if they were found worthy; the linings of the waistbands were inspected; of course the pockets of the pantaloons were turned inside out and their contents appropriated. The proceeds derived from this search were turned over to Wirz for temporary deposit, afterward to be divided fairly.

> "The squads were then turned over to the sergeants of the guard, and such miscellaneous articles as their superiors did not require, or did not desire to take, were appropriated. Thence they were passed to the outside guard to be marshaled into procession for the prison. If these last harpies found anything upon the persons of the prisoners worthy of their regard, it was incontinently taken, and by the time the poor wretches formed into column the regiment that Falstaff once raised would have shown well in comparison with these.

> "When they at last reached the stockade and were turned into the gates, the remnants that were left to them by the rapacious crew through whose hands they had passed were not sufficient to cover their nakedness. But there was slight comfort left the poor wretches in the reflection that they were no worse off than the 20,000 who had preceded them into this Gehenna of earthly misery and none of these could boast themselves of being possessed of more than themselves. The picture is but faintly drawn, as the author most willingly confesses that—"

But enough of this without wishing to hear Mr. Spencer's confession.

The above-named authors, after describing how everything was taken from the prisoners, go on to state that rebel sutlers enriched themselves by charging exorbitant prices for food, clothing, blankets, tobacco, liquors, and other articles sold to the prisoners!

How about the thousands of dollars, the watches and jewelry stolen by the marauders from the prisoners, and the prisoner who had his watch and $175 in greenbacks taken, if they had been despoiled of everything they had before entering the prison?

The Andersonville histories here mentioned are in every library of note north of the Ohio River, and the skeptic can investigate for himself as to the truth or falsity of the above statements.

Confederate Camp Sumter, 1864.
Courtesy of the National Archives.

Edward W. Boate

Chapter Four

A Federal Report (1865)

Edward Wellington Boate, a Federal soldier imprisoned in Andersonville, wrote this article for the *New York News* in July of 1865. This account, which is essentially the Southern view of the time, later appeared in Volume X, an 1882 edition, of the *Southern Historical Society Papers.* The Southern Historical Society, founded in 1869, included such luminaries as Robert E. Lee, Alexander Stephens, Dr. J. William Jones, and Wade Hampton. The *Southern Historical Society Papers* are available in reprint in fifty-five volumes (including a three volume index) and remain a favorite source for historical researchers.

The bread was badly baked, the bakery being run night and day; the ten thousand prisoners—the number originally intended to be confined at Andersonville—having risen to thirty-eight thousand, and, in addition to the fact that many of our men engaged in the bakery had very little sympathy with the poor men in the stockade, and took as little trouble with their work as possible, they were themselves over-tasked. Hence the bread was badly baked. Besides, our men were not used to corn bread, a fact which used to make the Georgians wonder, as they grew fat on corn bred, just as the healthiest and most able-bodied Irishman you could meet at a fair was a man whose principal food was potatoes.

The water was diarrheal—a fact which was as injurious to the health of the Confederate authorities in that locality as to our men. But this difficulty was partially obviated by the digging of innumerable wells in various parts of the prison, and excellent water obtained, which the well diggers monopolized and sold for a cent a glass to those who had no claim on the wells.

But our men were great sufferers, and deaths were alarmingly on the increase. The Confederate doctors were, as I have already said, themselves startled and alarmed at the progress of disease and death. But they seemed powerless to check it. I can honestly say—and every man who was connected with the hospital department will bear me out—that the twenty-five or thirty Confederate surgeons who were in attendance at the hospital and in the stockade, acted with as much humanity toward the prisoners as the disheartening circumstances would permit. We were often a fortnight without being able to get medicine. They had no quinine for fever and ague; they had no opium for diarrhea and dysentery. Our government made medicine a contraband of war, and wherever they found medicine on a blockade runner, it was confiscated, a policy which indicated, on the part of our rulers, both ignorance and barbaric cruelty; for, although no amount of medicine would save many of our men who have laid their bones in Georgia, I am as certain as I am of my own existence, that hundreds of men died, who, if we had had the right sort and proper quantity of medicine, would have been living to-day and restored to their families.

Scurvy was another disease which was making formidable inroads upon the health of the prisoners, but vegetables could not be had for love or money, although for miles the country was scoured, and I knew Chief Surgeon White to pay from a hundred to two hundred dollars for a quantity of squashes, collards, onions and other garden stuff which could have been purchased in Fulton or Washington market for five or six dollars; although a "greenback" in Andersonville rated at only four times the value of a Confederate dollar—at Richmond it was rated at ten and twelve Confederate dollars. These vegetables were necessarily, from their limited quantity, confined to the hospital. In addition to this the hospital was supplied with eggs, no doubt in limited quantities. [Three dollars in greenbacks for a dozen of eggs.] Fresh beef was supplied to the hospital two or three times a week, and sometimes to the stockade, when it could be had, cattle having for this purpose been sought for miles around the country.

The hospital and sick men in the stockade were supplied with whiskey, three and four barrels having been some days brought into headquarters, and regular details of our own men appointed to distribute it, who, however, often drank the rations themselves. The hospital was supplied with tea and sugar, not abundantly to be sure, but hospitals even in New York city, are not over-abundantly supplied with such articles.

Nevertheless, great misery prevailed in the stockade. But it was inevitable from the circumstances. The men, two out of every three, had no change of underclothing, and although there was water enough to wash them, they could not get soap, an article of which the Confederate authorities were themselves especially in need. The bodies of our men, and indeed the minds, had become prostrated from long confinement, in many instances sixteen and twenty months. There were gathered into one prison, by the force of events, nearly forty thousand men, to be provided with food, and five thousand with medicine. They were deprived of their accustomed food, and had to live upon the same kind of rations, day after day, nearly the whole of the time. But none, except those who have gone through the mill, know what a tremendous task it is to provide daily rations for such a vast multitude of human beings.

There are some special facts I wish to state of my own knowledge, as they will throw some light on this unhappy subject. It has been stated over and over, and reiterated in a thousand different shapes, that the Confederate authorities meant to starve our men. But I, who was twelve months a prisoner of war, and suffered sickness, and cold, and hunger, in common with the other prisoners, deny this flatly, for, while we all suffered, there was no desire to inflict suffering or hardship upon Federal prisoners. Why, the Confederate authorities were suffering many a privation at Andersonville. The surgeons who were in attendance upon the sick had not decent shoes or stockings; their shoes and boots being in many instances so patched, that the original leather out of which they had been manufactured had become invisible. These gentlemen, men of education and professional ability, and who were reared in luxury, did not know often—while giving their

Union prisoners dispersing dirt from an escape tunnel;
William H. Shelton, Artist. Courtesy of National Park Service.

services daily and nightly to such a host of prisoners—where to look
for a dinner or a bed. During the six months I was in Andersonville,
not one of them received a dollar's pay. The consequence was, that
they had been turned out of their boarding houses in the adjacent
villages and country houses, and Dr. White, head surgeon, had to provide quarters for them as best he might. These surgeons had often to
share the tents of the paroled Federal prisoners. Dr. White himself was
often glad to get even a share of the prison rations—corn bread and
ham—while engaged in his official and professional duties; often for
fourteen or fifteen hours without intermission. He was an able surgeon, humane, enlightened, abstemious and self-denying, and had all
the high-souled chivalry and deportment of the best of the F. F. V's.

In this connection, let me refer to Captain Wirz, the Commandant
of the prison, who was generally regarded as being very harsh. But his
position should be considered. He was a mere keeper of prisoners—a
work which can never be popular. The Yankees were nightly and indeed daily trying to run away, as they were bound to do; but he said

he was bound to catch them wherever he could find them. Between the jailer and the jailed, there could not and never can be any peculiar love; but, under a rough exterior, more often assumed then felt, this Captain Wirz was as kind-hearted a man as I ever met. Being myself at headquarters I learned his character, and the opinion I formed of him when in the stockade, which was one of a bitter kind enough, I had to change when I came really to know the man. The first collision between Captain Wirz and his prisoners was, when on the 17th of March he wanted to squad them off, for the purpose of exactly ascertaining the number of rations that would be needed at that date, the men wanted to play a flank movement, so as to get counted in two squads, and thereby get double rations. Half the prisoners were placed at the south side of the "swamp," the other at the north side. When the Confederate sergeants counted the squads at the north side, and dismissed each squad as counted and named, hundreds of them dodged across the "swamp" and got into the southern side squads by the time the sergeants were able to get across, in order to get double rations, giving different names to those they went by at the other side. But the number of prisoners sent into the stockade had been kept carefully at headquarters, and it was found that some two thousand had attempted the "flank movement," that is some two thousand more rations were returned on the count in the prison than could be accounted for. The trick was discovered, and as it was perpetrated on the north side the captain stopped their rations that day, but gave them to the south side of the prison.

This caused bad blood between the north side and the captain. The men groaned him when he entered, and henceforth there was an intermittent feud; but the men who attempted this trick ought to have known and done better. In quantity the rations were double, whatever other drawbacks there might have been.

Every night men worked at the tunneling from under some tent, out, under and at the other side of the stockade; but there was always some traitor in camp who informed on the "conspirators," just as the tunnel was completed. When discovered, the captain would ride in at the head of his guards and march to the exact spot where the tunnel was to be found. But, although nightly discovered, the men worked like beavers at "tunneling" in some other part of the camp; but I do not believe that a single one of those tunnels ever proved successful. The captain was thus kept in hot water, and being a man of a by no means mild temper, he often cursed and damned, but that was all.

Men were, however, nightly making their escape over the stockade, by bribing the guards, and by other dodges; and, though they often had a five hours' start, the hounds being sent in pursuit, they were almost invariably overtaken and brought back, when they were

Union memorial service, 1896.
Courtesy of the National Park Service.

for some days put in ball and chain, and sent back to the stockade; but they were no sooner inside than they managed to file off the ball and chain, only appearing in their (sham) pedal bracelets every morning during the counting of the men by the Confederate sergeants. As an evidence that Wirz was actuated by no desire to inflict hardship upon our men, I heard him often exclaim, when a new hatch of some five or six hundred prisoners would come: "I would as soon send these unfortunate men into h—l as into that d—d bull pen. It sickens me."

The men often arrived at the prison without a blanket or any sort of "kit;" and in they marched and had to make their lodging on the cold ground. At this time every branch and leaf for miles around had been cut down to make tents; and men had, when permitted to haul firewood, to go several miles around the country under guard. It often happened, by the by, that on these occasions the Federal soldiers would, when a sufficient distance from the stockade, lay hands on the guard, "buck and gag" him, take away his gun, and make their escape.

Many of the men were suffering sadly for want of tents to keep them from the fierce rays of the sun and the equally fierce rain which often fell for ten or twelve hours together. It will here be asked, as it has often been asked before, "Why did not the Confederate authorities at Andersonville give our men wooden huts in a woody country?" This question has been often asked, and never answered. Yet it can be fairly, if not quite satisfactorily, explained.

Day after day in May and June the papers were bringing us authentic reports that exchange was at hand. Exchange became a fixed fact for some time. The commissioners had met at City Point, and General Grant had gone to Fortress Monroe, and the basis of exchange, as arranged by the commissioners, had been approved by the Lieutenant-General. But disappointment was sure to follow, and no exchange was visible. At one period, during a long interval of disappointment, I saw a plan drawn up at headquarters for the erection of wooden barracks, so ingenious and comprehensive that 40,000 men could be conveniently housed in prison; and the wood was commenced to be cut down for the purpose. In mid-career an official report reached headquarters that exchange would be commenced in ten days from date, and wood-cutting was given up as superfluous. In a few weeks, toward the close of July, General Stoneman's raid at Macon took place, and the Confederates immediately commenced, with their available help of niggers, to fortify Andersonville, which they certainly believed was to be immediately attacked. At this very period Dr. White, who had started for Macon to hurry up medicine, was stopped at Fort Valley, half-way between Andersonville and Macon; and, instead of coming back with medicine, came to his office armed to the teeth, announcing to the surgeons that they must help to defend the place, according to the instructions of General Winder, as the prison was to be immediately attacked. We, Federal paroled prisoners, it was announced, were to be sent down to the hospital. The cannon planted around headquarters, which dominated the prison, were charged and manned, and everything ready for defense. During the previous week of rumors of attack, huge breast-works were thrown up by niggers who labored at them night as well as day. Stoneman was, however, himself captured, and the excitement passed away. Thoughts of changing the location of the prison occupied the minds of the authorities, as they did not know what moment the prison would be attacked and the prisoners carried off. Confusion, apprehension and dread filled the minds of the Andersonville officers.

Things, however, soon calmed down. A few weeks previously, a great movement had taken place in the prison. The great paramount idea of the prisoners was exchange. They accordingly called a great meeting, and after some preliminary proceedings, resolutions, and a memorial to President Lincoln, were adopted, asking, in view of the suffering and mortality of our men, that he should agree to an exchange of prisoners, as the Confederates were willing to exchange man for man and officer for officer, leaving the excess of prisoners at which ever side found. Six prisoners, including myself as Chairman, were appointed a Commission to proceed to Washington, and lay the whole question before the Executive. This was toward the close of August. After some negotiations with General Winder, the balance of twenty-one men due to our government, the six delegates being included, were permitted to come North; and on our way through Macon we met General Stoneman at Prison Oglethorpe, where the Federal officers were confined, and he gave us a letter to the President, strongly urging the necessity of exchange, not for the officers he said, but for the brave men who had fought so gallantly in the field, and suffered so much in prison, and begging the President to forego all idea of the exchange of negroes, if that were the point which stood in the way.

Down to Charleston. Arriving at Pocotaligo, we were exchanged—that is, nine out of the twenty-one, two of the commissioners being kept back, although the twelve not exchanged might as well have been as there were plenty Confederate prisoners at Beaufort, only a dozen miles away.

Arriving in New York, the four commissioners applied for the necessary transportation at General Dix's office. It was refused, although Colonel Hall, Deputy Provost Marshal at Hilton Head, had given us letters to the headquarters of the department of the east, stating our mission, etc. The Sanitary Commission, however, supplied the transportation, and three of the commissioners proceeded to Washington, I remaining, however, in this city through illness, although I was not idle. They wrote to the President, and reported the object of their visit on three consecutive days; but it distresses me to state *that the representatives of thirty-eight thousand Union prisoners were treated with silent contempt, the President declining to see them or have any communication with them !!!*

For obvious reasons I shall be silent as to the motive of President Lincoln in his treatment of the delegation. But I cannot help stating that the lives of some ten or twelve thousand men might have been spared had an exchange justly, I will not add generously, taken place at this period.

From February to the end of August there were some six thousand deaths at Andersonville from various causes, circumstances and diseases. This number, I understand, before exchange took place, or our government consented to do so, reached some fifteen or sixteen thousand.

General Winder remarked to us before we quitted Andersonville, that the object of our government in refusing to exchange was that they felt it hard to give soldiers for civilians. "The time," added he, "of thousands of those unhappy men in that stockade is out many months; thousand of others are rendered worthless for soldiers through long confinement, disease and privations—for I will admit that we have not the resources to treat your men as we would wish."

Since I returned to the North, Winder's words were confirmed, for it was semi-officially stated to me that, "It might look very hard that we refused to exchange; but we could not afford to do so. We would have to give a number of strong, well fed, available soldiers for a number of men broken down from campaigning, disease, and out of the service by the expiration of their term."

A policy like this is the quintessence of inhumanity, a disgrace to the Administration which carried it out, and a blot upon the country. You rulers who make the charge that the rebels intentionally killed off our men, when I can honestly swear they were doing every thing in their power to sustain us, do not lay this flattering unction to your souls. You abandoned your brave men in the hour of their cruelest need. They fought for the Union, and you reached no hand out to save the old faithful, loyal, and devoted servants of the country. You may try to shift the blame from your own shoulders, but posterity will saddle the responsibility where it justly belongs.

Dedication of the New York Monument on April 29, 1914. Original photographer: J. G. Waters. Courtesy of the National Park Service.

The Union Dead at the South Gate.
Courtesy of the National Park Service.

Mildred Lewis Rutherford

Chapter Five

Correspondence Regarding Henry Wirz, Commander of Andersonville Prison (1921)

Mildred Lewis Rutherford, venerable Grand Historian of the United Daughters of the Confederacy, enthralled audiences coast-to-coast with her fiery orations defending the Old South. "Miss Millie," an Athens, Georgia teacher and writer, published a number of historical pamphlets during the early 1900's This particular collection of correspondence pertaining to Captain Wirz was printed in a January, 1921 UDC bulletin compiled by Miss Rutherford and entitled *Facts and Figures vs. Myths and Misrepresentation: the Truth About Captain Wirz*

Correspondence Regarding Commander of Andersonville Prison, Who Was Tried and Executed in Washington in 1865. Championed by Late Louis Schade. (From *The Washington Post*).

A great deal of interest was expressed yesterday among some of the old inhabitants of Washington regarding the protest entered at Minneapolis by the G. A. R. Convention against the erection of a monument in memory of Captain Henry Wirz, commander of Andersonville Prison during the Civil War. The trial and execution of Wirz took place in Washington in 1865, and the intense feeling which characterized this trial is still remembered.

A reporter of *The Post* called on H. R. Schade, son of the late Louis Schade, defender of Wirz at his trial. Mr. Schade, when asked what he thought of the action of the G. A. R., said he was, in a measure, surprised at the position taken by the old veterans regarding this matter; he called attention to the fact that a monument was about to be erected at Harpers Ferry in memory of John Brown, and no protest had been heard from the South in regard to the erection of such a monument.

Mr. Schade stated that he had for some months been in correspondence with a number of prominent Georgians, and that he was now preparing a magazine article pertaining to the trial of Wirz, and that the proceeds of this article would be contributed to the Wirz monument fund. He added, however, that he did not care to express an opinion regarding the trial and execution of Wirz, but preferred to let the statement issued by his father, made in 1867, and a letter written by Jefferson Davis in 1888, speak for themselves. He thought that the letters addressed to President Johnson and to his father by Wirz were in themselves sufficient defense; he thereupon furnished the reporter copies of these letters. The letters were as follows:

"Washington, D. C., April 4, 1867.
"To the American public:

"Intending to leave the United States for some time, I feel it my duty before I start to fulfill in part a promise which, a few hours before his death, I gave to my unfortunate client, Captain Wirz, who was executed at Washington on the 10th day of November, 1885. Protesting up to the last moment his innocence of those monstrous crimes with which he was charged, he received my word that, having failed to save him from a felon's doom, I would as long as I lived do everything in my power to clear his memory. I did that the more readily as I was then already perfectly convinced that he suffered wrongfully. Since that time his unfortunate children, both here and in Europe, have constantly implored me to wipe out the terrible stains which now cover the name of their father.

"Though the times do not seem propitious for obtaining full justice; yet, considering that man is mortal, I will, before entering upon a perilous voyage, perform my duty to those innocent orphans, and also to myself. I will now give a brief statement of the causes which led to the arrest and execution of Captain Wirz. In April, 1865, President Johnson issued a proclamation stating that from evidence in the possession of the Bureau of Military Justice, it appeared that Jefferson Davis was implicated in the assassination of Abraham Lincoln, and for that reason the President offered a reward of $100,000 for the capture of the then fugitive ex-President of the Southern Confederacy. (A copy of the paper containing this offer is in Athens. Ga.) That testimony has since been found to be entirely false and a mere fabrication, and the suborner, Conover, is now under sentence in the jail in this city, the two perjurers whom he suborned having turned state's evidence against him, whilst the individual by whom Conover was suborned has not yet been brought to justice.

ENEMIES IN HIGH PLACES.

"Certain high and influential enemies of Jefferson Davis, either then already aware of the character of the testimony of those witnesses, or not thinking their testimony quite sufficient to hang Mr. Davis, expected to find the wanting material in the terrible mortality of Union prisoners at Andersonville. Orders were issued accordingly to arrest a subaltern officer, Captain Wirz, a poor, friendless, and wounded prisoner of war (he being included in the surrender of General Johnston), and, besides, a foreigner by birth. On the 9th day of May he was placed in the Old Capitol Prison at Washington, and from that time the greater part of the Northern press busily engaged in transforming the unfortunate man, in the eyes of the Northern people, into such a monster that it became almost impossible for him to obtain counsel. Even his countryman, the Swiss consul general, publicly refused to accept money or defray the expenses of the trial. He was doomed before he was heard, and even the permission to be heard according to law was denied him. To increase the excitement, and give eclat to the proceeding, and to influence still more the public mind, the trial took place under the very dome of the Capitol of the nation.

"A military commission, presided over by one of the most arbitrary and despotic generals in the country, was formed, and the paroled prisoner of war, his wounds still open, was so feeble that he had to recline during the trial on a sofa. How that trial was conducted the whole world knows. The enemies of generosity and humanity believed it to be a sure thing to get at Jefferson Davis. Therefore, the first charge was that of conspiracy between Wirz, Jefferson Davis, Seddon, Howell Cobb, R. B. Winder, R. R. Stevenson, and a number of others to kill the Union prisoners.

"The trial lasted for three months, but, fortunately for the blood-thirsty instigators, not a particle of evidence was produced showing the existence of such a conspiracy, yet Captain Wirz was found guilty of that charge. Having thus failed, another effort was made. On the night before the execution of the prisoner, a telegram was sent to the Northern press from this city, stating that Wirz had made important disclosures to General L. C. Baker, the well known detective, implicating Jefferson Davis, and that the confession would probably be given to the public. On the same evening some parties came to the confessor of Wirz, Rev. Father Boyle, and also to me, one of them informing me that a high Cabinet officer wished to assure Wirz that if he would implicate Jefferson Davis with the atrocities committed at Andersonville his sentence would be commuted. The messenger, or whoever he was, requested me to inform Wirz of this. In the presence of Father Boyle, I told Wirz next morning what had happened.

WIRZ REFUSES BRIBE OF LIFE.

"The captain simply and quietly replied: 'Mr. Schade, you know that I have always told you that I do not know anything about Jefferson Davis. He had no connection with me as to what was done at Andersonville. If I knew anything about him, I would not become a traitor against him, or anybody else, even to save my life.' He likewise denied that he had ever made any statement whatever to General Baker. Thus ended the attempt to suborn Captain Wirz against Jefferson Davis. That alone shows what a man he was. How many of his defamers would have done the same? With his wounded arm in a sling, the poor paroled prisoner mounted, two hours later, the scaffold. His last words were that he died innocent; and so he did.

"The 10th day of November, 1865, will indeed be a black stain upon the pages of American history. To weaken the effect of his declaration of innocence, and of the noble manner in which Wirz died, a telegram was manufactured here and sent North, stating that on the 27th day of October Mrs. Wirz (who actually was 900 miles on that day away from Washington) had been prevented by that Stantonian Deus ex machina, General L. C. Baker, from poisoning her husband. Thus, on the same day when the unfortunate family lost their husband and father, a cowardly and atrocious attempt was made to blacken their character also. On the next day I branded the whole as an infamous lie, and since then I have never heard of it again, though it emanated from a brigadier general of the United States army.

"All those who were charged with having conspired with Captain Wirz have since been released, except Jefferson Davis, the prisoner of the American 'Castle Chillon.' Captain Winder was let off without a trial, and if any of the others have been tried, which I do not know, certainly none of them has been hung. As Captain Wirz could not conspire alone, nobody will now, in view of that important fact, consider him guilty of that charge. So much, then, for charge No. 1.

THE ANDERSONVILLE CHARGES.

"As to charge No. 2, to wit, murder, in violation of the laws and customs of war, I do not hesitate to declare that about 145 out 160 witnesses on both sides declared during the trial that Captain Wirz never murdered or killed any Union prisoners with his own hands or otherwise. All those witnesses (about twelve or fifteen) who testified that they saw Captain Wirz kill a prisoner have sworn falsely, abundant proofs of that assertion being in existence. The hands of Captain Wirz are clear of the blood of prisoners of war. He would certainly have at least intimated to me a knowledge of the alleged murders with which he was charged. In almost all cases, no names of the alleged murdered men could be given, and where it was done, no such persons could be identified. The terrible scene in court when he was confronted with one of the witnesses, and the latter insisted that Wirz was the man who killed a certain Union prisoner, which irritated the prisoner so much that he almost fainted, will still be remembered. That man (Grey) swore falsely, and God alone knows what the poor, innocent prisoner must have suffered at that moment. That scene was depicted and illustrated in the Northern newspapers as if Wirz had broken down on account of his guilt. Seldom has a mortal suffered more than that friendless and forsaken man. Fearing lest this communication should be too long, I will merely speak of the principal and most intelligent of those false witnesses, who testified to individual murder on the part of Captain Wirz.

A PERJURED WITNESS.

"Upon his testimony the judge advocate, in his final argument, laid particular stress, on account of his intelligence. This witness prepared also pictures of the alleged cruelties of Wirz, which were handed to the commission, and are now on record, copies of which appeared at the time in Northern illustrated papers. He swore that his name was Felix de la Baume, and represented himself as a Frenchman and grand-nephew of Marquis Lafayette. After having so well testified and shown so much zeal, he received a recommendation signed by the members of the commission. On the 11th day of October, before the taking of the testimony was concluded, he was appointed to a clerkship in the Department of the Interior. This occurred while one of the witnesses for the defense (Duncan) was arrested in open court and placed in prison before he had testified. After execution of Captain Wirz, some of the Germans of Washington recognized in de la Baume a deserter from the Seventh New York (Steuben's) Regiment, whose name was not de la Baume, but Felix Oeser, a native of Saxony. They went to Secretary Harlan, and he dismissed the impostor, the important witness in the Wirz trial, on the 21st day of November, eleven days after the execution. Nobody who is acquainted with the Conover testimony, in consequence of which the President of the United States was falsely induced to place a reward of $100,000 upon the head of an innocent man, will be astonished at the disclosures of the character of testimony before military commissions. So much for charge 2.

LACK OF MEDICINE BLAMED.

"If from twelve to fifteen witnesses could be found who were willing to testify to so many acts of murder on the part of Wirz, there must certainly have been no lack of such who were willing to swear to minor offenses. Such was the unnatural state of the public mind against the prisoner at that time that such men regarded themselves and were regarded as heroes, after having testified in the manner above described; while, on the other hand, the witnesses for the defense were intimidated, particularly after one of them had been arrested.

"But who is responsible for the many lives that were lost at Andersonville and in the Southern prisons? That question has not fully been settled, but history will tell on whose heads the guilt for those sacrificed hecatombs of human beings is to be placed. It was certainly not the fault of poor Captain Wirz, when, in consequence of medicines having been declared contraband of war by the North, the Union prisoners died for the want of the same. How often have we read during the war that ladies going South had been arrested and placed in the old Capitol Prison by the Union authorities because some quinine or other medicine had been found concealed in their clothing? Our navy prevented the ingress of medical stores from the seaside, and our troops repeatedly destroyed drug stores and even the supplies of private physicians in the South. Thus, the scarcity of medicines became general all over the South.

PROVISIONS VERY SCARCE.

"That provisions in the South were scarce will astonish nobody, when it is remembered how the war was carried on, Gen. Sheridan boasted in his report that, in the Shenandoah Valley alone, he burnt over 2,000 barns, filled with wheat and corn, and the mills in the whole tract of country; that he destroyed all factories of cloth, and killed or drove every animal—even the poultry—that could contribute to human sustenance. And these desolations were repeated in different parts of the South, and so thoroughly that last month, two years after the end of the war, Congress had to appropriate $1,000,000 to

"View from Wirz's Headquarters of the Stockade
at Andersonville," from sketch by R. K. Sneden.
Courtesy of the National Park Service.

save the people of those regions from actual starvation. The destruction of railroads and other means of transportation by which food could be supplied by abundant districts to those without it increased the difficulties in giving sufficient food to our prisoners. The Confederate authorities, aware of their inability to maintain their prisoners, informed the Northern agents of the great mortality, and urgently requested that the prisoners should be exchanged, even without regard to the surplus which the Confederates had on the exchange roll from former exchanges—that is, man for man. But our War Department did not consent to an exchange. They did not want to 'exchange skeletons for healthy men.'

"Finally, when all hopes of exchange were gone, Colonel Ould, the Confederate commissioner of exchange, offered, early in August, 1864, to deliver up all Federal sick and wounded, without requiring an equivalent in return, and pledged that the number would amount to 10,000 or 15,000; and if it did not, he would make up that number from well men. Although this offer was made in August, the transportation was not sent for them (to Savannah) until December, although he urged and implored (to use his own words) that haste should be made. During that very period most of the deaths at Andersonville occurred. Congressman Covode, who lost two sons in Southern prisons, will do well if he inquires who those 'skeletons' were which the honorable Secretary of War (Stanton) did not want to exchange for healthy men. If he does he will hereafter perhaps be less bitter against the people of the South.

'MILITARISM' CONDEMNED.

"We used justly to proclaim in former times that ours was the 'land of the free and the home of the brave.' But when one-half of the country is shrouded in despotism which now only finds a parallel in Russian Poland, and when our generals and soldiers quietly permit that their former adversaries shall be treated worse than the Helots of old, brave soldiers though they may be, who, when the forces and resources of both sections were more equal, have not seldom seen the backs of our best generals, not to speak of such men as Butler and consorts, then we may question whether the Star-Spangled Banner still waves 'o'er the land of the free and the home of the brave.'

"A noble and brave soldier never permits his antagonist to be calumniated and trampled upon after an honorable surrender. Besides, notwithstanding the decision of the highest legal tribunal in the land, that military commissions are unconstitutional, and earnest and able protestations of President Johnson, and the sad results of military commissions, yet such military commissions are again established by recent legislation of Congress all over the suffering and starving South. History is just, and, as Mr. Lincoln used to say, 'We cannot escape history.' Puritanical hypocrisy, self-adulation, and self-glorification will not save these enemies of liberty from their just punishment. Not even a Christian burial of the remains of Captain Wirz has been allowed by Secretary Stanton. They still lie side by side with those of another and acknowledged victim of military commissions, the unfortunate Mrs. Surratt, in the yard of the former jail of this city. If anybody should desire to reply to this, I politely beg that it may be done before the 1st of May next, as I shall leave the country, to return in the fall. After that day, letters will reach me in care of the American legation, or Mr. Benedetto Bolzani, Leipzig street, No. 38, Berlin, Prussia.
"LOUIS SCHADE, "Attorney at Law."

It would seem after this overwhelming testimony from the North no other would be needed.

The South made every effort to send the prisoners home to relieve the congested condition at the prison, and to place them where proper care should be taken of them, and medicine administered, but the Federal authorities refused every offer.

(See General Lee's request for exchange).

(See Alexander Stephens' request for exchange).

(See Colonel Ould's offer to fill a vessel with sick or well prisoners without exchange).

(See petition of the paroled prisoners).

(See effort by Confederate Government to send prisoners home without any exchange).

(See order to Adj. John C. Rutherford to march a body of these prisoners across the Florida line and to leave them).

Series II., Vol. VIII., *The War of Rebellion.*

All facts can be found in the Official Records of *The War of the Rebellion,* Series I., II., IV.

The United Daughters of the Confederacy
Memorial to Captain Henry Wirz, C.S.A.

PRAISE FROM JEFFERSON DAVIS.

"Beauvoir, Miss., October 15, 1888.
"Louis Schade, Esq.

"My Dear Sir: I have often felt with poignant regret that the Southern public have never done justice to the martyr, Major Wirz. With a wish to do something to awake due consideration for his memory, I write to ask you to give the circumstances, as fully as may be agreeable to you, of the visit made to him the night before his execution, when he was tempted by the offer of a pardon if he would criminate me, and thus exonerate himself of charges of which he was innocent, and with which I had no connection.

"Respectfully and truly yours,
"JEFFERSON DAVIS."

WIRZ THANKS MR. SCHADE.

"Old Capitol Prison,
"Washington, D. C., Nov. 10, 1865.
"Mr. Louis Schade.

"Dear Sir: It is no doubt the last time that I address myself to you. What I have said to you often as often I repeat. Accept my thanks, my sincere, heartfelt thanks, for all you have done for me. May God reward you, I cannot. I still have something more to ask of you, and I am confident you will not refuse to receive my dying request. Please help my poor family—my dear wife and children. War, cruelest, has swept everything from me, and today my wife and children are beggars. My life is demanded as an atonement. I am willing to give it, and hope that after a while, I will be judged differently from what I am now. If any one ought to come to the relief of my family, it is the people of the South, for whose sake I have sacrificed all. I know you will excuse me for troubling you again. Farewell, dear sir. May God bless you.

"Yours thankfully,
"H. WIRZ."

WIRZ APPEALS TO THE PRESIDENT.

"Old Capitol Prison,
"November 6, 1865.
"To the President of the United States.

"Mr. President: With a trembling hand, with a heart filled with the most conflicting emotions, and with a spirit hopeful one moment and despairing the next, I have taken the liberty of addressing you. When I consider your exalted position; when I think for a moment that in your hands rests the weal or woe of millions—yea, the peace of the world—well may I pause to call to my aid courage enough to lay before you my humble petition. I have heard you spoken of as a man willing and ready at all times and under all circumstances to do justice, and that no man, however humble he may be, need fear to approach you; and, therefore, have come to the conclusion that you will allow me the same privilege as extended to hundreds and thousands of others. It is not my desire to enter into an argument as to the merits of my case. In your hands, if I am rightfully informed, are all the records and evidences bearing upon this point, and it would be presumption on my part to say one word about it. There is only one thing that I ask, and it is expressed in few words: Pass your sentence.

"For six weary months I have been a prisoner; for six months my name has been in the mouth of every one; by thousands I am considered a monster of cruelty, a wretch that ought not to pollute the earth any longer. Truly, when I pass in my mind over the testimony given, I sometimes almost doubt my own existence. I doubt that I am the Captain Wirz spoken of. I doubt that such a man ever lived, such as he is said to be; and I am inclined to call on the mountains to fall upon and bury me and my shame. But oh, sir, while I wring my hands in mute and hopeless despair, there speaks a small but unmistakable voice within me that says: 'Console thyself, thou knowest thy innocence. Fear not; if men hold thee guilty, God does not, and a new life will pervade your being.' Such has been the state of my mind for weeks and months, and no punishment that human ingenuity can inflict could increase my distress.

GIVE ME LIBERTY OR GIVE ME DEATH.

"The pangs of death are short, and therefore I humbly pray that you will pass your sentence without delay. Give me death or liberty. The one I do not fear; the other I crave. If you believe me guilty of the terrible charges that have been heaped upon me, deliver me to the executioner. If not guilty, in your estimation, restore me to liberty and life. A life such as I am now living is no life. I breathe, sleep, eat, but it is only the mechanical functions I perform, and nothing more. Whatever you decide I shall accept. If condemned to death, I shall suffer without a murmur. If restored to liberty, I will thank and bless you for it.

"I would not convey the idea to your mind, Mr. President, that I court death. Life is sweet; however lowly or humble man's station may be, he clings to life. His soul is filled with awe when he contemplates the future, the unknown land where the judgment is before which he will have to give an account of his words, thoughts, and deeds. Well may I remember, too, that I have erred like all other human beings. But of those things for which I may perhaps suffer a violent death, I am not guilty; and God judge me. I have said all that I wished to say. Excuse my boldness in addressing you, but I could not help it. I cannot bear this suspense much longer. May God bless you, and be with you; your task is a great and fearful one. In life or death I shall pray for you, and for the prosperity of the country in which I have passed some of my happiest as well as darkest days.

Respectfully,
"H. WIRZ."

GENERAL TAYLOR'S STATEMENT.

Lieutenant General Richard Taylor, son of President Zachary Taylor and brother-in-law of President Davis, has this to say of Wirz, in his very interesting book, *Destruction and Reconstruction*:

"In this journey through Georgia, (1864) at Andersonville, I passed in sight of a large stockade inclosing prisoners of war. The train stopped for a few minutes, and there entered the carriage, to speak to me, a man who said his name was Wirz, and that he was in charge of the prisoners near by. He complained of the inadequacy of his guard and of the want of supplies as the adjacent region was sterile and thinly populated. He also said that the prisoners were suffering from cold, were destitute of blankets, and that he had not wagons to supply fuel. He showed me duplicates of requisitions and appeals for relief that he had made to different authorities and these I indorsed in the strongest terms possible, hoping to accomplish some good. I know nothing of this Wirz, whom I then met for the first and only time. but he appeared to be earnest in his desire to mitigate the conditions of his prisoners. There can be but little doubt that his execution was a 'sop' to the passions of the 'many-headed.'"

This is the testimony given by Dr. Jos. Jones, a surgeon sent to investigate the conditions existing at Andersonville Prison, and this portion of his report was mutilated and never read at the trial of Wirz.

"Camp Sumter, Andersonville,
"September 17, 1864.

"Captain H. Wirz.
"You will permit Surgeon Joseph Jones, who has orders from the Surgeon-General, to visit the sick within the stockade to make certain investigations.

"By direction of GEN. WINDER,
Assistant Adjutant General"

War of Rebellion, Series II., Vol. VIII., p. 589.
SURGEON JONES' REPORT (Extracts).

"I carefully analyzed the waters; found them all remarkably pure. The well of water upon the summit of the hill upon which the Confederate General Hospital is situated, is of remarkable purity, and in fact it may be considered as equal to the purest water in the world. The waters of the Sweetwater Creek before entering into the stockade where the Federal prisoners are confined, are equally pure.

"The bakery is situated near this stream, and while one of the Confederate regiments is camped on the hill above, these sources of contamination is too far distant to affect the constant flowing waters.

"The water from all sources flowing into the stockade is remarkably pure, but that flowing from the stockade are loaded with filth and emit a sickening odor, disgusting and overpowering.

"The vegetation of the highlands and hills indicate poverty of soil. The lowgrounds and swamps bordering the streams are clothed with pines and oats of stunted growth. From this examination there is no recognizable source of disease in the soil and waters of Andersonville.

"After examination I was impressed with the belief that this region of country was as healthy as any region of the world situated in the same latitude and at the same elevation above the sea and that this locality chosen by the Confederates for the confinement of Federal prisoners, was much more salubrious than most of the region in Georgia lying to the south and southeast of it.

The heat caused the rapid decomposition of filthy matter in the stockade area, and this may have been a cause of debility—but the awful mortality must have been due to other causes—crowded condition and lack of medicine rather than to all the elements of climate combined.

"No blame can be attached to the Confederate authorities for this great mortality at Andersonville.

"In this collection of men from all parts of the civilized world every phase of human character was represented. The stronger preyed upon the weaker, and even the sick, who were unable to defend themselves were robbed of their scanty supplies of food and clothing. Dark stories were afloat of men murdered at night, strangled to death by their comrades for clothing or money. I heard a wounded Federal prisoner accuse his nurse, a fellow prisoner, of having inoculated his arm with gangrene in order to destroy his life to fall heir to his clothing.

The haggard, distressed countenances of these miserable, complaining, dejected, living skeletons, crying for medical aid and food, and cursing their Government for its refusal to exchange prisoners, and the ghastly corpses, with their glazed eye-balls staring up into vacant space, with flies swarming down open mouths formed a picture of helpless, hopeless misery which it would be impossible to portray by word or brush. As many men as possible were paroled and allowed to follow trades.

"The police and hygiene of the hospital was defective in the extreme, but no blame should be attached to the Confederate Government, to the commanding officer or to the Confederate guards.

"Scurvy was not confined to the prisoners. I saw a well-defined case of scurvy in a surgeon in care of one of the hospitals."

This report of Dr. Joseph Jones may be found in full in Series II., Vol. VIII., *War of Rebellion* pp. 590-632.

A UNION SOLDIER'S TRIBUTE TO MAJOR WIRZ.

(Macon News, March, 1907).

A letter received by Mrs. L. G. Young, wife of General L. G. Young, recently, throws light on the conduct of Major Wirz at Andersonville from a standpoint entirely different from that of the many Northern histories that have been written, and of the evidence that came out of the trial of Major Wirz at Washington.

The letter is the outcome of an article that a gentleman in Helena, Mont., read in *The Confederate Veteran,* in which it was stated that Mrs. Young was the originator of the movement to erect a monument at Andersonville to the memory of Major Wirz. The gentleman is now writing a history of Andersonville Prison, in conjunction with a friend of his who was there during seven months of the time that Major Wirz was charged with having accomplished all of the foul deeds charged to him. The letter is as follows:

"Dear Madam: By *The Confederate Veteran* for October I see that you were the lady who took the initiative in erecting a monument to Major Wirz and I take the liberty of writing you for information.

"A friend of mine, an influential and respected citizen of Montana, was for seven months a prisoner at Andersonville. He was orderly sergeant in a Michigan regiment when captured, and some twelve or fifteen years ago he told me that Wirz was a kind-hearted man who did everything in his power to alleviate the condition of the prisoners under him.

"This was a revelation to me. My friend had sort of charge over about 100 of the prisoners, and was also one of a committee who frequently waited on Major Wirz. He told me that twice Wirz burst into tears when told of the suffering of the prisoners. Once, late in 1864, Wirz said, 'God help you, I cannot. What can I do? I cannot make provisions. My own men have not enough to eat. They are now on short rations.'

"For years I have been after my friend to write his version of Andersonville. A year ago he consented to do so. He and I are now at the work. He is a prominent member of the G. A. R. I have recently collected excellent data from *The Confederate Veteran*. (This book was The "True History of Andersonville" by Page and Haley.)

DAUGHTER OF MAJOR WIRZ.

"The contradictory accounts in Glazier's, Kellogg's Spencer's and Urban's (Union Soldiers) histories of Andersonville furnishes good material. Ours will also be from a Northern standpoint. There will, however, be this difference: ours will be a true account. Those other histories were untruthful.

"Will you please kindly inform me if Major Wirz 's daughter is still living, and if so where does she live?

"Do you know the address of Dr. R. Randolph Stevenson who wrote *The Southern Side of Andersonville*? I have tried, but cannot get the book.

"Dear Mrs. Young, any information that you can give me I assure you will be most thankfully received. You might be able to give me the address of parties who were cognizant of the facts, those who were in close touch with Major Wirz.

"Our Northern historians claim that Wirz put men to death, but the very fact that prisoners themselves were obliged to execute six of their fellow prisoners is presumptive evidence that death had to be resorted to to maintain order and discipline.

"During the last dozen years my friend has repeatedly told me that while confined at Andersonville—and he was there during the latter part of it—he never heard nor never knew that Wirz personally killed a prisoner, and that the 'killing' only came out at the trial. Said he: 'The Wirz I knew at Andersonville and the Wirz tried at Washington were two different persons.' There's a volume in that.

"The title of our book will be *Major Wirz Vindicated,* or *Andersonville As It Was,* or perhaps, *Fact, Not Fiction of Andersonville.* We have not yet determined what the title will be."

The letter was signed by M. L. Haley, No. 819 Fifth Avenue, Helena, Mont., and an answer will be sent by Mrs. Young, giving all the information possible.

This letter, coming as it does from the close friend of a man who went through the enforced horrors of the Confederate prison at Andersonville, telling of the conditions there that were not the fault of Major Wirz, is highly prized here, and has been turned over to the Daughters of the Confederacy.

Strong sentiment against the erection of the proposed monument at Americus instead of at Andersonville has arisen here, and it has been positively decided that it will be erected at Andersonville as near the spot where the old prison stood as possible.

General Young, who is deeply interested in the movement, as well as Mrs. Young, said yesterday that he had received letters from all over the country asking that the monument be erected as originally proposed, at Andersonville.

ANDERSONVILLE THE PLACE.

The proposed change in the location of the monument was for the reason, it was argued, that if erected at Andersonville it would be the cause of friction whenever Northern visitors paid a visit to the cemetery where their dead were buried. It was even stated that if the monument were erected at Andersonville that it would be torn down, and threats were made to this effect, anonymously.

But for all of these letters General Young says the place for the monument is at Andersonville, and there it shall go. He has received letters from a number of Confederate veterans stating that if the monument were erected at Andersonville they would volunteer their services to protect it so long as they might live.

"Let them tear it down," said General Young. "We will build it up again, and whenever they lay their fingers of desecration upon it the blood of the entire South will be aroused, and a larger, grander and more appropriate shaft will be constructed to the memory of this much maligned man."

"The Execution of Henry Wirz, November 10, 1865,
Adjusting the Rope." Courtesy Library of Congress
and the National Park Service.

Captain Henry Wirz, A.A.G., C.S.A.
Commander of Camp Sumter Prison,
(Andersonville), Georgia, 1864-1865.
Born 25 November 1823, Zurich, Switzerland
Executed 10 November 1865, Washington, D.C.
Buried Mount Olivet Cemetary, Washington, D.C.
Picture: 1863, Baden, Switzerland
(Wirz Family Archives)

Part Two

Contemporary Analysis

98   *The Journal of Confederate History*

Postwar rendering of Andersonville Prison.
Courtesy of the Georgia Department of Archives and History.

William R. Scaife

Chapter Six

Andersonville and Sherman's Campaign for Georgia

William R. Scaife is the author of *The Campaign for Atlanta*, *The War in Georgia*, and *Hood's Campaign for Tennessee* and has written feature articles for *Blue and Gray Magazine* and *Campaign Chronicles*. This historian, a former officer in the 82nd Airborne, and registered architect and professional engineer, is a frequent speaker and battlefield tour guide for a number of organizations to include the Atlanta Historical Society and the Atlanta Civil War Round Table. Bill Scaife is considered by many to be the foremost authority on Sherman's campaigns in Georgia.

One of the primary considerations in choosing Andersonville for such a large military prison was its remote location. Deep in the piney woods of south Georgia, and readily accessible only by rail, it was considered quite secure from enemy raids because of the great distances separating it from any active military operations of the Federal forces. But in May of 1864, General William T. Sherman began a campaign into Georgia which would take him from Ringgold in the extreme northeast corner of the state, to Savannah on the Atlantic coast, and would bring his marching columns within 65 miles of Andersonville. But only once during that uninvited guest's 8 1/2 months in Georgia did he attempt to free the prisoners incarcerated at Andersonville—and that attempt ended in humiliating failure.

As Sherman's forces approached Atlanta in early July, Andersonville came within raiding range of his cavalry, and on July 11, 1864, Confederate General Joseph E. Johnston wisely recommended removal of the prisoners to a more secure location. [1] Johnston bashing revisionist historians like to contend Johnston's recommendation was proof that he intended to evacuate Atlanta without a fight—but, in truth, it was a prophetic precaution against the cavalry raid that did actually begin only 16 days later, on July 27. Known as the *Great Cavalry Raid*, or the Stoneman-McCook Raid, Sherman's plan was to send three divisions of almost 10,000 picked cavalry in a deep pincer movement to the south of Atlanta on July 27. Edward M. McCook's division was to strike from the west, crossing the Chattahoochee River below Campbellton, while George Stoneman's and Kenner Garrard's divisions struck from the east—all three divisions converging on Lovejoy's Station, 26 miles below Atlanta on the evening of July 28. They would then proceed southward to Macon, destroying the Macon & Western Railroad as they went.

Before the raid got under way, George Stoneman requested permission to continue fifty miles southwest of Macon to Camp Sumter, the Confederate prisoner of war camp better known as Andersonville, to attempt to liberate the 30,000 Federal prisoners confined there. Apparently charmed with the idea, Sherman agreed to the Andersonville mission and telegraphed General Halleck in Washington on July 16:

> "I send by the right a force of about 3,500 cavalry under General McCook, and round by the left about 5,000 cavalry, under Stoneman, with orders to reach the railroad about Griffin. I also have consented that Stoneman, if he finds it feasible, may with his division proper, go to Macon and attempt the release of our officers prisoner there, and then to Andersonville to release 20,000 of our men there. This is probably more

than he can accomplish, but it is worthy of a determined effort"[2]

Sherman then dispatched Stoneman:

"You may, after having fulfilled my present orders, send General Garrard back to the left flank of the army, and proceed with your command proper to accomplish both or either of the objects named [Macon or Andersonville].......if you can bring to the army any or all of those prisoners of war, it will be an achievement that will entitle you and the men of your command to the love and admiration of the whole country. " [3]

Neither Sherman nor Stoneman apparently gave much thought to how 30,000 weak and emaciated men could make their way on foot through 100 miles of hostile territory to reach the Federal lines, once they had been freed by Stoneman's cavalrymen.

Stoneman apparently became obsessed with freeing the prisoners and becoming an instant national hero and took it upon himself to go to Andersonville first, free the prisoners, then return and destroy the railroad in accordance with Sherman's orders. But he neglected to inform Garrard or McCook of his intended deviation from the original plan and in so doing, doomed the entire mission to failure.

The raid got under way on the morning of July 27, McCook crossing the Chattahoochee River and heading through Palmetto and Fayetteville toward Lovejoy's Station, while Garrard moved to Flat Rock on the South River—where he was to join Stoneman and then proceed to the rendezvous with McCook at Lovejoy's. McCook, with the brigades of John T. Croxton, William H. Torrey and Thomas J. Harrison, crossed the Chattahoochee on a pontoon bridge at Smith's Ferry, six miles below Campbellton. The 1st Wisconsin Regiment of Torrey's brigade screened McCook's left flank during the operation and was attacked by Colonel Thomas H. Harrison's (Confederate) brigade of William H. Jackson's cavalry. The 1st Wisconsin's commander, Major Nathan Paine, was killed and his regiment driven back across the Chattahoochee, but the diversion enabled McCook's main force to cross the river undetected.

By noon on July 27, Confederate General Joseph Wheeler had detected the massive Federal movement and sent John H. Kelly with the brigades of Colonel George G. Dibrell and Colonel Robert H. Anderson to intercept Garrard, who was encamped on Snapfinger Creek, near the point where it entered South River. Since Garrard had been ordered to remain near Flat Rock and wait for Stoneman to join him, he pulled back to Latimer's Corner, now the community of Belmont on

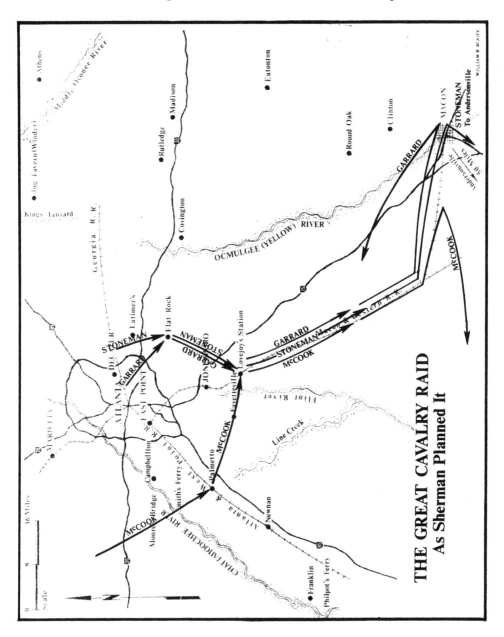

THE GREAT CAVALRY RAID
As Sherman Planned It

the Covington Highway, and remained there. Wheeler then learned that Stoneman, with another division was moving toward Macon and, shortly thereafter, received word from General Hood's headquarters that still another large cavalry force (McCook) was moving around the Confederate left and appeared too large to be checked by General William H. Jackson's under-strength division of cavalry. Wheeler reacted quickly. Leaving George D. Dibrell's brigade with John H. Kelly at Latimer's Corner to watch Garrard, he sent Alfred Iverson with Iverson's own brigade, William Wirt Allen's and William C. P. Breckinridge's brigades, to pursue Stoneman in the direction of Macon, while Wheeler moved with Henry Ashby's and Robert H. Anderson's brigades to the west to help Jackson contend with McCook.

The western half of the great Federal *pincer* movement under General Edward M. McCook proceeded to Palmetto with Torrey's brigade in the lead, followed by Croxton and Harrison. They tore up some two miles of railroad and telegraph lines at Palmetto, then continued along the Fayetteville Road, where they encountered a long Confederate wagon train. They captured some 300 guards and wagoners, burned 500 wagons and killed the horses and mules with their sabres, least gunfire divulge their presence to the enemy.

Lieutenant Granville C. West of the 4th Regiment of Kentucky (Federal) Mounted Infantry of Croxton's brigade described the butcher of the animals:

> "Whenever a soldier saw a chance to make an advantageous trade in horses he generally did so, if he had time to make the change, otherwise he was likely to run his sword or sabre through the neck or heart of the horse or mule and leave him dead or disabled, and hundreds of them were thus sabred, maimed or killed. It may be said that this was cruel. Admitted. No one denies that it was cruel. But it was war, and war is cruel."[4]

McCook continued eastward through Fayetteville, across the Flint River to Lovejoy's Station, the appointed rendezvous with Stoneman and Garrard, arriving there at 7:00 a.m. on July 29. His troopers destroyed railroad track and telegraph lines near Lovejoy's until 2:00 p.m., when McCook learned that Wheeler's cavalry was between his position and McDonough, from which direction he expected Stoneman and Garrard to approach Lovejoy's Station. McCook therefore decided to return to the Chattahoochee River by way of Fayetteville and Newnan and moved out with Torrey's brigade, under Colonel Horace Lamson, in the lead, followed by Colonel Thomas J. Harrison's brigade, with Colonel John T. Croxton's brigade bringing up the rear. [5]

Wheeler took out after McCook's retreating column and pursued it relentlessly, with Lawrence S. Ross' Texas Brigade swinging in from the northeast in an attempt to separate Croxton's rear brigade from the main column, while Wheeler, with Henry M. Ashby's brigade, pressed from the rear. McCook's men, who had little or no sleep for two days and nights, were nearing exhaustion. Some fell asleep in the saddle and weary horses and mules could scarcely be coaxed along. Large numbers of Confederate prisoners from the captured wagon train, which accompanied McCook's column, escaped and others misled their captors into taking wrong turns at critical crossroads. About mid way between Fayetteville and Newnan and three miles west of Line Creek, Colonel Henry M. Ashby's brigade overtook McCook's rear guard of the 4th Kentucky Mounted Infantry. Lieutenant Granville C. West, who commanded the 4th Kentucky, described how they were overtaken and surrounded, but still managed to avoid capture:

> "The light of the morning disclosed the enemy in every direction, and swarming about us the force in my front had come up in speaking distance. The officer in command bawled out to me, 'SURRENDER YOU DAMN YANKEE!,........With scornful contempt, I told him to, 'GO TO HELL!,.........I raised my sword and pointed in the direction of the way to go—for an order could not be heard in the strife—and put the spurs to my horse. It was a reckless move but the effect was instantaneous. A convulsive tremor, a rush, and, in defiance of a chorus of demands to surrender, we were out, and away, and gone." [6]

McCook had hoped to find temporary refuge from Wheeler's ha - rassing attacks in the town of Newnan, but was in for yet another surprise. Brigadier General Philip D. Roddey's 550 man brigade of dismounted cavalry had been moving by rail from Mississippi to reinforce Hood's army in Atlanta, but was stranded in Newnan when McCook destroyed the Atlanta & West Point Railroad at Palmetto on July 28. As the advance units of McCook's column, Company D and Company E of the 8th Indiana Regiment of Harrison's brigade, moved into Newnan, they were confronted by Roddey's Brigade in line of battle and driven from town. McCook therefore decided to bypass Newnan to the south, along a narrow, twisting route called the Ricketyback Road. But Wheeler continued his aggressive pursuit, sending Colonel Henry M. Ashby with about 200 men of the 2nd and 5th Tennessee regiments through Newnan and down the LaGrange (now Old Corinth) Road to intercept the head of McCook's column—while Wheeler, with Ross' and part and Harrison's brigades moved southward to strike the column in flank.

BATTLE OF BROWN'S MILL

Torrey's brigade led McCook's column with the 2nd Kentucky Regiment on the point, followed by the 4th Indiana, then the pack train, ambulances and prisoners, followed by the 3 inch ordnance rifles of Lieutenant Martin Miller's 18th Indiana Battery of Horse Artillery and finally the 2nd Indiana Regiment. The 8th Iowa, 4th Kentucky, and 1st Tennessee regiments of Croxton's brigade followed, then the 4th Tennessee and 5th Iowa regiments of Harrison's brigade, followed by the rear guard of the 8th Indiana Regiment. When the head of the column reached the LaGrange Road, it was struck hard by Colonel Henry M. Ashby's Confederates and the three leading regiments were scattered. Major George H. Purdy of the 4th Indiana Regiment led the survivors of the 4th Indiana, 2nd Indiana and the 4th Kentucky to the northwest some 15 miles to the Chattahoochee River, where they crossed about 20 miles below Moore's Bridge and eventually made their way back to Marietta.

The scattering of Torrey's lead brigade left Lieutenant Martin Miller's Horse Artillery near the head of the column, where they unlimbered their two 3 inch ordnance rifles and fired canister into Ashby's attackers until their ammunition was exhausted. They then spiked the guns, chopped the carriages and limbers to pieces with axes, and the artillerymen mounted the battery mules and fled to the south.

Ross' Texas Brigade struck Croxton's brigade in the center and Thomas H. Harrison s Confederate brigade struck Thomas J. Harrison's Federal brigade at the rear of the column with such ferocity that McCook summoned his brigade commanders and instructed each to try to break out wherever possible, in an, "every man for himself," operation.

Colonel James P. Brownlow led the 1st Tennessee and 4th Kentucky of Croxton's brigade through the encirclement to the northwest and crossed the Chattahoochee near Campbellton. But when Colonel Croxton went back to direct the 8th Iowa along the same route, he found the regiment had been cut to pieces and all had been killed or captured except Major Richard Root, Captain John Dance, Lieutenant Jackson Morrow and 10 privates. Colonel Croxton then found himself cut off and only by abandoning his horse and hiding in the woods, was able to avoid capture and eventually escape to the Federal lines, on foot.

Colonel Thomas J. Harrison, who commanded the trailing brigade in McCook's column, was surrounded and forced to surrender with 60

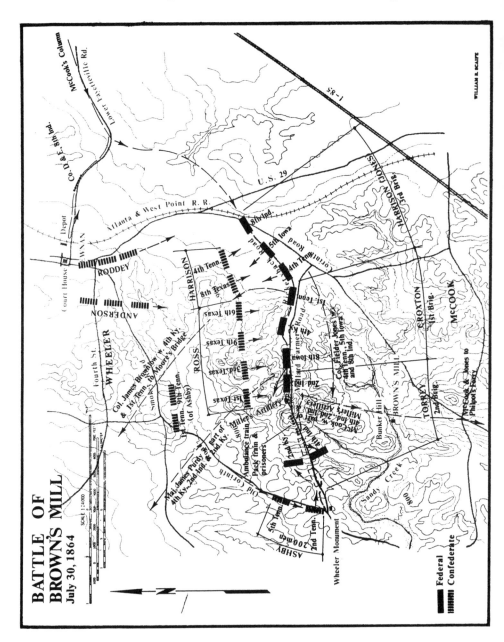

BATTLE OF
BROWN'S MILL
July 30, 1864

officers and men. Colonel Fielder A. Jones extricated what was left of Harrison's brigade and fled first to the south, then to the west—where he joined McCook with what was left of the 2nd and 4th Indiana regiments and Martin Miller's mule-mounted cannoneers. McCook's and Jones' combined forces crossed Sandy Creek in the vicinity of Brown's Mill,[7] a mile south of the battlefield, and fled to the southwest, crossing the Chattahoochee at Philpot's Ferry, south of Franklin—and finally reaching Marietta six days later.

Edward M. McCook's report on the engagement at Brown's Mill was brief and to the point:

> "I was finally completely surrounded, and compelled to abandon everything that would impede me in order to cut my way through. I ordered Colonels Croxton and Torry [Torrey] to cut through with their brigades. I took Colonel Jones with me and got through 1200 men, by a charge in column, and crossed the river below Franklin. Colonel Dow, Colonel Torry and Major Austin were wounded; Major Paine killed; Colonel Harrison missing, supposed to be a prisoner. My loss heavy. No co-operation from Stoneman."[8]

Joseph Wheeler's dispatch from Newnan following the battle was even briefer than McCook's, but could hardly have covered the subject more lucidly:

> "We have just completed the killing, capturing and breaking up the entire raiding party under General McCook."[9]

In the meantime, George Stoneman's command, which formed the east wing of the great *pincer* movement, left Decatur on the morning of July 27. His force consisted of the 5th and 6th Indiana regiments brigaded under Colonel James Biddle, the 1st and 11th Kentucky regiments under Colonel Silas Adams, the 14th Illinois, 8th Michigan and part of the 1st Ohio Squadron under Colonel Horace Capron and a section of the 24th Indiana Battery of Artillery with two 3 inch ordnance rifles—a total force of 2,112 men, including Stoneman and a personal staff of seven.[10] They crossed the Ocmulgee (Yellow) River near Conyers, then continued to the southeast toward Macon along the east bank of the Ocmulgee River, passing through Covington on July 28 and Monticello on the 29th.

The town of Griswoldville had been established 10 miles east of Macon on the Georgia Central railroad during the 1840's by industrial entrepreneur, Samuel Griswold. The small manufacturing community contained a pistol factory which turned out Colt Navy Repeaters, a brick plant, saw mill, soap, candle and furniture factories and several

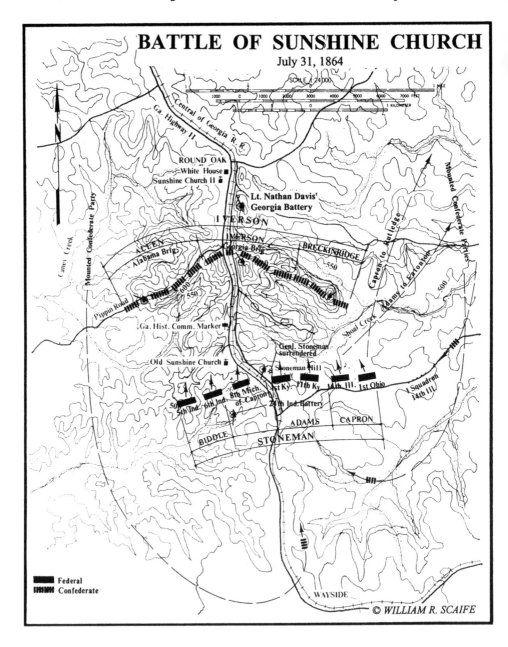

BATTLE OF SUNSHINE CHURCH
July 31, 1864

© WILLIAM R. SCAIFE

hundred houses for workers and slaves. As Stoneman approached the area, one of Griswold's slaves, a negro named Minor, ran away and joined the Federal cavalry force, offering his services as a guide. With the aid of his new found guide, Stoneman embarked on a spree of burning and pillaging along the Georgia Central Railroad east of Macon, doing extensive damage to the railroad, rolling stock and private property in and near the communities of Gordon, Emmet Station, McIntyre and Toombsboro.

On July 30, Stoneman concentrated his division and advanced on Macon from the east, but when he reached Dunlop's Farm on the high ground east of the Ocmulgee River, was confronted by General Howell Cobb with a force of Georgia Militia and home guard units, entrenched with artillery support. Stoneman decided against attacking such a formidable position and ordered his division to bypass Macon and to move southward in the direction of Andersonville. But General Howell Cobb had a trick up his sleeve, intentionally allowing several of his pickets to be captured—each of whom, upon interrogation, told their captors the same story—that some 1500 Confederate cavalrymen were entering Macon to reinforce the garrison. At that point Stoneman appears to have lost his zeal for freeing the prisoners at Andersonville and turned his entire column northward in the direction of Clinton, and unknowingly, directly into the face of Alfred Iverson's pursuing Confederate forces.

BATTLE OF SUNSHINE CHURCH

As Stoneman approached the small hamlet of Round Oak, some 18 miles north of Macon, on July 31, he found Alfred Iverson's division drawn up and waiting for him. Iverson was from nearby Clinton and Wheeler had selected him to lead the mission in pursuit of Stoneman because of his familiarity with the area between Macon and Atlanta. He had selected his ground well, on a ridge just north of Sunshine Church, where the gently rolling terrain suddenly became more rugged, with several deep ravines running perpendicular to the road. He formed his men in an inverted "V" with the open end facing Stoneman and placed his artillery, under Lieutenant Nathan Davis, in the center and on the flanks. Stoneman first tried to overrun Iverson's position and escape to the north, but the "V" configuration of the Confederate line forced Stoneman's troops toward the center, where they received an ever increasing enfilading fire from both sides. Iverson then sent several small mounted parties southward around Stoneman's flanks, where they then turned and came galloping northward into the Federal rear, shooting and yelling as they went. Stoneman assumed they were the imaginary horseman he had been told about at Macon and concluded that he was surrounded. At 4:00 p.m. Stoneman assembled his staff and brigade commanders and informed them that he would himself remain with Biddle's brigade as a rear guard and hold off the enemy until Adams and Capron could move to the right and north and escape with their brigades. Just as Stoneman was issuing his final instructions, Iverson's Confederates mounted a general attack along the entire line, causing Silas Adams' brigade, in Stoneman's center, to suddenly break for the rear. Colonel Horace Capron described the fiasco that followed:

> "The sudden retreat of Adam's brigade opened a wide gap in our line, through which the enemy plunged in a wild rush toward the rear, where our horses were. The men of my brigade for a few minutes maintained their alignment, meanwhile casting wistful glances toward their horses Nothing is more demoralizing to a cavalryman fighting dismounted as to find his horse in danger of capture. In the race for their possession every man had opportunity to notice his pitiable condition, encumbered with heavy cavalry boots, as the nimble-footed infantrymen passed him in the race. When he reflected that he was a hundred miles in rear of the enemy's lines, with an immense army interposed between him and freedom, he wanted his horse, and many a man lost his life in trying to get one. MY KINGDOM FOR A HORSE!" [11]

Adams and Capron fled to the east, then turned north and escaped, while Stoneman remained with Biddle's rear guard. Stoneman was captured on the hill which now bears his name near the center of the battlefield, along with Colonel James Biddle, Minor, his negro guide, and almost 600 officers and men. The Confederates immediately hanged Minor, from the nearest tree and were preparing the same fate for Stoneman when Confederate officers halted the execution. Stoneman is said to have openly wept when told after his capture that he had surrendered to a force little over half the size of his own. [12] He was sent to Macon, where he remained a prisoner of war until exchanged in September for Confederate Brigadier General Daniel C. Govan. On August 6, Stoneman wrote Sherman from his prison cell in Macon:

> "Without entering into particulars, we were whipped.....My own horse had been shot under me and I was scarcely able to mount the only one I could find to replace the one I had lost, and our chances of escape were so small that I consented to be taken a prisoner of war, and as such, our treatment has been everything that could be expected........I feel better satisfied to be a prisoner of war, much as I hate it, than to be amongst those who owe their escape to considerations of self-preservation." [13]

Adams' and Capron's brigades fled northward, Adams by way of Eatonton and Capron by Rutledge, rejoining forces at Madison on

August 1 and proceeding on toward Athens. But when they were confronted by Captain Edward P. Lumpkin's *Mitchell Thunderbolts*, at the bridge over the Middle Oconee River four miles southwest of Athens, both brigades turned to the west, Capron by the Hog Mountain Road to Jug Tavern (now Winder), while Adams bore north until he finally reached the Federal lines at Marietta on August 4.

Capron passed through Jug Tavern and encamped about five miles to the northwest at King's Tanyard, sending Major Francis M. Davidson's battalion of the 14th Illinois a mile to his rear as pickets. Several hundred negro refugees had followed Capron's column, apparently expecting some measure of protection from the Federal cavalry, and bivouacked between Capron's main camp and Davidson's pickets.

BATTLE OF KING'S TANYARD

Iverson's Confederates clung tenaciously to the rear of the fleeing Federals, with Colonel William C. P. Breckinridge's Kentucky Brigade in the lead. During the night of August 2, Breckinridge halted and selected 85 men with the freshest horses and sent them ahead under Major Richard Bowles, with orders to attack the enemy wherever found. Just before dawn on August 3, Major Bowles' advance party surprised Capron's sleeping men and stampeded them, along with the negro refugees camped nearby, in what was known as the Battle of King's Tanyard. Most of Capron's brigade was captured and Capron himself reached the Federal lines four days later, on foot. He later penned a vivid account of his Odyssey, which read in part:

> "I had scarcely lost consciousness in sleep, when I was suddenly aroused by the most unearthly yells and screams, mingled with pistol shots. It appears that a considerable force of the enemy came up with our rear....flanked Davidson's picket, which was probably asleep, and charged directly across the negro camp upon us. Every darkey, mule, horse and donkey were driven pel-mell upon our poor, worn out troops. Brave men as ever drew a sabre in battle ran past their officers in a confused, frenzied mass towards the bridge [over Mulberry Creek]. As the crowd poured upon it, the bridge gave way with a crash, followed by the cries of the wounded men. Then commenced another haphazard ride, which not only tried the mettle of our steeds, but our own nerves as well. Ditch after ditch, fence after fence, was scaled, thickets of briers and scrubby trees were brushed through at breakneck speed, while now and then a rifle ball cut the branches from around us, but the thoughts of the terrible suffering in a rebel prison-pen had by far the most powerful influence to stimulate us to renewed exertion." [14]

While both Stoneman and McCook's divisions were being effectively destroyed by Wheeler's cavalry, Kenner Garrard remained relatively inactive with his force of some 3,500. Since his orders had been to remain near Flat Rock until joined by Stoneman, he took no initiative even when it became obvious that Stoneman was not going to put in an appearance. Garrard explained in his report:

> "They [the Confederates] showed no line of battle, and would fall back as we advanced, and then follow to observe us. My examinations did not take the body of my command near the railroad, and to break the road would require three or four days. I did not deem it advisable to attempt it." [15]

Both Stoneman and McCook had broken communications with the main Federal army during the raid and as Sherman waited anxiously, the bad news began to trickle in. The first of McCook's command to come in was Colonel Brownlow, who arrived at Marietta during the night of July 31 with only 28 men, followed by Major Purdy on August 1, with 280 men of Torrey's brigade. On August 1, Sherman telegraphed General Halleck in Washington:

> "Colonel Brownlow reports that he reached Marietta, having escaped from the disaster that overtook McCook's expedition at Newnan. After a hard fight McCook had to surrender. I can hardly believe it, as he had 3,000 picked cavalrymen." [16]

On August 4, Colonel Silas Adams arrived from Stoneman's command with only 490 men and on August 5, McCook came in with the remnants of Torrey's brigade, accompanied by Colonel Fielder A. Jones with what was left of Harrison's brigade and the men of Miller's artillery, unceremoniously mounted on the battery mules. Colonel Capron came in on foot on August 7 and Colonel Croxton and his orderly arrived shortly thereafter, also on foot.

Colonel Israel Garrard, who assumed command after Stoneman's surrender at Sunshine Church, reported losses in the Great Raid of 10 killed, 26 wounded and 1,229 missing out of an original force of 2,112, or 58 percent. McCook filed no report of casualties but official returns on August 8 reported 1,139 Total Present for Duty, with only 536 Mounted and Equipped, out of an original force of 3,600—indicating a loss of 2,461, or 68 percent. Kenner Garrard's lack of initiative had saved his division from all combat, save some light skirmishing and official returns for August 8 gave his strength as 3,528 Total Present for Duty—substantially the same as were reported before the raid started.[17]

The *Great Cavalry Raid* had ended in the most spectacular Confederate victory of the campaign and enough horses were captured from Stoneman's command alone to allow Joseph Lewis' Kentucky *Orphan Brigade* to be fully mounted at Palmetto in September. General Joseph Wheeler summed up the Great Cavalry Raid in two sentences:

> "This proved to be a picked body of cavalry, and its destruction destroyed the flower of Sherman's vast cavalry organization. Thus ended in ignominious defeat and destruction, the most stupendous cavalry operation of the war." [18]

Sherman's dispatches left little doubt as to his reaction to the *Great Cavalry Raid*. On August 2, he wrote George H. Thomas:

> "I am quite unwell today. Please do all that is possible to organize a force of cavalry about Marietta, composed of Kilpatrick's division and such of General McCook's as have returned." [19]

On August 7, he wrote General Halleck in Washington and came about as near as he would ever come to apologizing for his actions:

> "In order that you may have a proper understanding of the recent cavalry operations from this army that terminated somewhat unsuccessfully, I will explain.....Nothing but the natural and intense desire to accomplish an end so inviting to one's feelings [release of the prisoners at Andersonville] would have drawn me to commit a military mistake, at such a crisis, as that of dividing and risking my cavalry, so necessary to the success of my campaign." [20]

Thus Sherman's only attempt to free the prisoners at Andersonville resulted in the most humiliating defeat suffered during his campaign in Georgia and almost totally annihilated his cavalry corps. In his official report, written some six weeks later, Sherman summarized the ill-fated expedition:

> "I estimated this joint cavalry could whip all of Wheeler's cavalry, and could otherwise accomplish its task, and I think so still. His [Stoneman's] mistake was in not making the first concentration with Generals McCook and Garrard near Lovejoy's, according to his orders, which is yet unexplained. General McCook is entitled to much credit for saving his command, which was endangered by the failure of General Stoneman to reach Lovejoy's. But on the whole the cavalry raid is not deemed a success...." [21]

Many question why Sherman never made a greater effort to free the prisoners at Andersonville, for he certainly had favorable opportunities to do so. On September 1, Sherman's entire army was concentrated near Jonesboro, with only William J. Hardee's single battered and exhausted corps of Confederates at Lovejoy's Station lying between him and Andersonville. But Sherman elected to retire into Atlanta, to rest his army and savor his conquest of the city.

In his memoirs, Sherman dismisses the Andersonville question rather lightly:

> "On the 22nd of September, I wrote to general Hood, describing the condition of our men at Andersonville, purposely refraining from casting odium on him or his associates for the treatment of these men, but asking his consent for me to procure from our generous friends at the North, the articles of clothing and comfort which they wanted...." [22]

Sherman reported that General Hood promptly consented, and he telegraphed the Sanitary Commission in St. Louis to send the supplies. But the prisoners were removed before these items arrived.

Sherman apparently was concerned with more pressing matters than freeing these hapless men, and the singular abortive effort discussed in this article appears to have been made solely on the recommendation of George Stoneman, rather than due to the humanity of William T. Sherman.

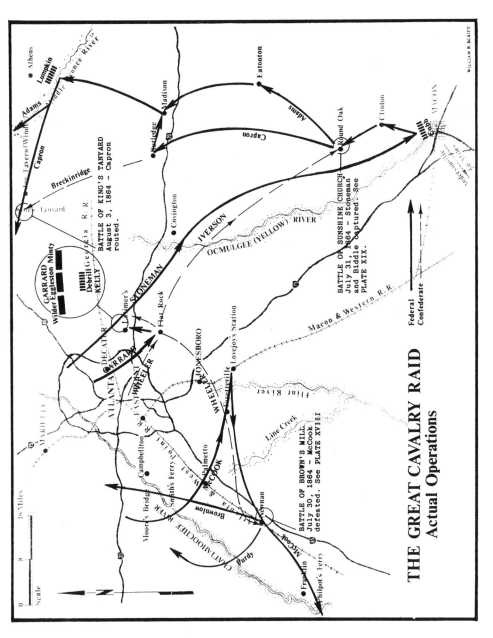

THE GREAT CAVALRY RAID
Actual Operations

NOTES

1. O. R. 38, V, 876.

2. O.R. 38, V, 260, Sherman to Halleck.

3. Ibid., 265, Sherman to Stoneman.

4. West, Granville C., "McCook's Raid in the Rear of Atlanta and Hood's Army," *MOLLUS*, 1898, D.C. Commandery.

5. O.R. 38, II, 762, McCook's Report and 769, Croxton's Report.

6. West, Granville C., "McCook's Raid in the Rear of Atlanta and Hood's Army," *MOLLUS*, 1898, D.C. Commandery.

7. Wheeler's attack on McCook's column on July 30 became known, perhaps for lack of a better landmark, as the *BATTLE OF BROWN'S MILL*.

8. O.R. 38, II, 762, McCook's Report.

9. O.R. 38, III, 689, Shoup's Journal.

10. O.R. 38, II, 915, Robert W. Smith's Report.

11. Capron, Horace, "Stoneman's Raid to the South of Atlanta," *MOLLUS*, 1899, D.C. Commandery.

12. Williams, Carolyn White, *HISTORY OF JONES COUNTY< GEORGIA*, 147.

13. O.R. 38, II, 914, Stoneman to Sherman under flag of truce from prison at Camp Oglethorpe in Macon.

14. Capron, Horace, "Stoneman's Raid to the South of Atlanta," *MOLLUS*, 1899, D.C. Commandery.

15. O.R. 38, II, 810, Kenner Gerrard's Report.

16. O.R. 38, V, 320, Sherman to Halleck.

17. O.R. 38, I, 432, Effective Force of Cavalry, August 8, 1864 and II, 925, Israel Garrard's Report.

18. O.R. 38, III, 957, Wheeler's Report.

19.   O.R. 38, I, 330, Sherman to Thomas.

20.   O.R. 38, V, 409, Sherman to Halleck.

21.   O.R. 38, I, 77, Sherman's Report.

22.   *MEMOIRS*, II, 143.

Lee Joyner

Chapter Seven

Life in the Stockade

Earvin Lee Joyner, Jr. is currently writing a history of Andersonville. Educated at nearby Georgia Southwestern College in Americus, Joyner taught history for fourteen years in Georgia schools, worked as a Park Ranger and Historical Interpreter at Andersonville National Historic Site, and served as Assistant Historian for the upcoming Turner film production of *Andersonville*. An avid Civil War memorabilia collector, Joyner holds one of the largest private collections of primary source material, photographs, and relics relating to Andersonville.

"Sunday, August 21, 1864. A rainy and gloomy day. Nothing to eat as usual. It cannot last long this way. This evening, drew double rations;   was so weak could hardly stand up to get them. Made a small supper, and laid down to sleep at dark."[1]

Private Edward T. Abbott, Company H, 20th Connecticut Volunteer Infantry Regiment had endured life in Georgia's Andersonville Prison for nearly a month when he scribbled the entry into his battered diary. Captured at Atlanta, Georgia on July 23, 1864, Abbott and a number of other federal soldiers were marched to Griffin at which place they were loaded onto cattle cars, "sixty-five in a car...." After a stopover in Macon, the densely packed train reached Andersonville on the twenty-eighth. Private Abbott's sojourn in Confederate Camp Sumter, better known as Andersonville, was typical of the average soldier's life there.

The first prisoners to arrive at the prison were former occupants of Belle Isle, a prison surrounded by the waters of the James River at Richmond. Shipped in by rail, these men arrived at Andersonville just before the end of February. Taken off the train in the small village, they were marched over to the unfinished stockade by Confederate guards. These initial inmates of the prison were herded inside the log enclosure where they faced the muzzles of Confederate cannons which had been placed as a security precaution between the two gates where the wall had not yet been completed. In one month, the Andersonville stockade would become the home for nearly seven thousand men, most of whom were in weakened condition from their incarceration at Richmond. Their numbers would soon grow. With the closing of several other prisons in nearby states and the coming spring and summer campaigns in Georgia and Virginia, the prison soon became an overcrowded pen of misery and death. Nearly 33,000 Northern soldiers would eventually be crammed inside Andersonville by late summer of 1864. The enlargement of the stockade to encompass an additional ten acres was accomplished earlier in the season, but overcrowding remained one of the major problems. One prisoner likened it to a massive ant hill with the occupants swarming like the small insects.

Guard towers known as "pigeon roosts" lined the walls of the prison and earthen forts bristling with artillery were strategically located around the stockade to discourage prisoner uprisings and defend the post in the event of attack by Union forces. Veteran Confederate units, and later Georgia Reserves composed largely of inexperienced boys and older men, manned these towers with orders to shoot any prisoners venturing over the "Deadline," a small waist high rail fence about twenty feet from the inner wall and running the entire length and width of the prison. The deadline, as some authors contend, was peculiar to Andersonville. In truth both sides employed deadlines to keep prisoners "in line." At Johnson's Island Prison on Ohio's frigid Lake Erie, where numerous Confederate prisoners succumbed to disease and were frozen to death, a deadline was used by post authorities. [2]

Commander Wirz and his predecessor, Colonel Persons of the 55th Georgia Infantry both tried to improve the conditions of the camp and met with only limited success. A lack of cooperation from local sawmill operators in providing needed lumber for construction of shelter, commissary agents more concerned with lining their own pockets than providing quality meat for enemy prisoners, bureaucratic red tape, an overburdened and nearly broken down rail system laboring to move needed men and material to the front as well as sustenance to Southern soldiers, citizens and Yankee prisoners, and indifferent political figures on both sides contributed to the problem. The two camp commanders left behind a paper trail that reveals an honest effort was indeed made by those in charge to improve the prisoner's lot under their charge. However, numerous requests to governmental agencies for needed supplies were frequently ignored or passed over by the proper authorities.

Some of Camp Sumter's prisoners were transferred from other Confederate prisons; others had been recently taken on the battlefield or on board an unfortunate ship. They came dressed in rags or newly issued blue uniforms. Many were young, others middle-aged. Some spoke little English, their families having migrated from Europe only recently. The healthy, the infirm, the educated and the illiterate,...from the cities and farms of the North, West and South they came. Civilian teamsters, at least one known woman, drummer boys, black soldiers and their white officers, and Zouaves dressed in colorful uniforms copied from the French all passed through the heavy wooden gates of Andersonville.

From the opening of the camp in February through August the prison population, as we have seen, continued to rise. With the fall of Atlanta in early September most of the remaining prisoners were shipped to other camps, most notably Camp Lawton near Millen, Georgia. A skeleton force of guards remained behind to guard the remaining prisoners, most of whom were deemed too weak to be moved safely. By the late Spring of 1865 nearly all the remaining garrison along with their former charges were gone. Captain Wirz, believing himself to be covered under the terms of surrender signed by Generals Sherman and Johnston remained at the prison with his wife and daughters, little knowing he would soon be placed under arrest by a vindictive Northern government.

Thousands of prisoners at Andersonville died of diseases such as smallpox, dysentery, scorbutus (scurvy), diarrhea, pneumonia and a host of others. Overcrowded conditions, filthy water, and exposure to the elements weakened the constitutions of many. Medicine and qualified medical personnel were in short supply in Confederate Georgia, and Andersonville was certainly no exception. The medical staff of the garrison labored under horribly unsanitary conditions and were even known to use concoctions derived from local flora and fauna in lieu of precious supplies of quinine, morphine and other contraband medicines. Although their efforts were valiant, the huge load of weakened and sick prisoners was simply too great for all to receive proper medical attention. Some prisoners died on board crowded trains while being transported to other locales; others died on their way home after having been released; and a few expired shortly after seeing home and loved ones the final time.

"Andersonville Prison, Camp Sumter, Ga., as it appeared August 1, 1864, when it contained 35,000 prisoners of War," drawn from memory by Thomas O'Dea, late private, Co. E, 16th Regt. Maine Inft. Vols. Courtesy of the Library of Congress and National Park Service.

A number of these Union prisoners lived to be old men, and, eventually published their prison memoirs. These surviving diaries and letters provide glimpses into how the captives and their keepers truly lived at the Andersonville Prison. For example, Private Austin A. Carr, Company F, and later C, 82nd New York Volunteer Infantry Regiment, was captured at Petersburg, Virginia on June 22,1864 along with all but one company of his unit. In excerpts from his diary, he describes his train trip from Virginia to Andersonville: "...We reached a depot in Chester, S.C. stopping a half hour before being packed into freight cars like a herd of cattle....The train left South Carolina traveling very slowly to Augusta, Ga. The air was stifling. Many of our boys dying while enroute. The heat was...oppressive.... A young lady said as we passed through Georgia that 'The Yankees had all ought to have their throats cut.... The rebels stripped us of everything, even our blankets, leaving nothing to protect us from the bitter weather...." [3] Private Joseph Morris of Company G, 23rd Kentucky Volunteer Infantry Regiment, was captured in November at Nashville, Tennessee and was transported to Andersonville. His experiences, given to a New York officer shortly after the war are similar to Carr's. "He was entirely stripped of clothing and a few old rags given him—but not sufficient to cover his nakedness." [4] Nevertheless, other prisoners shipped by rail to Camp Sumter fared much better at the hands of their captors. Historical accounts show that the Federal garrison captured at Plymouth, North Carolina in the Spring of 1864 arrived at Andersonville with newly issued uniforms and equipment in addition to coveted greenbacks they had been recently paid by the government. How the prisoners and their property were treated depended chiefly on the Confederate troops guarding them.

The first contingent of prisoners that came to Andersonville picked up pine branches and limbs left behind by the slaves and fashioned makeshift shelters called shebangs. A crude set of barracks would be built later in the year, but for the most part prisoners had to provide their own shelter. Many dug caves in the clay walls of the north slope overlooking Stockade Branch, a sluggish stream that flowed listlessly across the width of the compound and was meant to provide water for all the prisoners' needs. Some prisoners dug pits in the earth and covered them with old blankets, overcoats, ponchos or brush. Those fortunate enough to have shelter halves fastened them together over wooden tent poles for protection from the elements. Many of these prison domiciles were quite large and could accommodate a number of men, while others were barely large enough for a single prisoner. Amos E. Stearns of Company A, 25th Massachusetts Infantry Regiment was made a prisoner on May 16,1864 at Drewry's Bluff, Virginia and spent a brief stay in Richmond's Libby Prison before being sent to Andersonville. He describes his arrival at the Georgia prison; "...The huge gate was opened and we passed in like so many sheep, with only the blue heavens above for shelter. The place assigned us was a low, marshy piece of ground near the creek...but we had to put up with it ...until we got places elsewhere among the prisoners." Stearns was not long without shelter as a comrade provided him room in his shebang following the death of a former tentmate. He continued, "Champney's shebang consisted of two army blankets fastened together with wooden pins, and put up like an A tent which, with a rubber poncho for the end, made a comfortable shelter compared with what the majority of them had for ...at this time there were so many prisoners in the stockade that hundreds of them had no shelter at all but had to lie on the ground...."[5]

Much has been written about the rations issued to the prisoners at Andersonville. In truth it can be said that the authorities simply weren't prepared to supply enough food for the thousands of prisoners in their care. The prison bakehouse ran night and day baking sheets of cornbread called cards which were issued to detachments of 270 men, which broke down into messes of 90 men, each under a federal sergeant's command. The sergeants procured the unbolted bread and frequently meal from a wagon that entered the South gate, usually on a daily basis. Before the ration was issued to the men, every man in a mess was assigned a number from one to ninety. When a soldier's number was called out by the sergeant, he approached the blanket or log where the food had been laid out on the ground to procure his ration. The cornbread frequently was of a very poor quality with the husk and cob of the corn ground up in the meal. Soldiers having no vessels in which to carry or cook the raw meal ate it as issued. Beef, pork, rice, yams, peas, molasses and salt were issued in varying quantities and qualities. Some soldiers complained of bugs in their peas. Charles Smedley of Company G, 90th Pennsylvania Volunteer Infantry Regiment was captured at the Wilderness, Virginia battle on May 5, 1864. He had been taken prisoner once before at Second Manassas two years earlier but was paroled shortly thereafter. On July 2, 1864 from inside Andersonville, Smedley wrote in his diary; "Was very hot until three o'clock P.M., when we had a heavy thunderstorm. Our little house let the rain in almost like a riddle...our detachment is now number thirty two, and my mess is the second mess. We got no rations until this evening, when we received meal, boiled and raw beef, and pork. Bread and salt were issued; we got raw beef and miserable bread, with a pinch of salt. We made a pot of mush for our breakfast, coffee and stewed meat for supper; we eat only twice a day. My disease (diarrhea) has left me and I am stouter." [5] On August 4 he writes, "Did not draw rations until this morning, when we got beans and half a ration of bread. This evening drew half a ration of bread, salt, and a very small ration of beef. Had beef and bean soup for supper; nothing to eat before of any account." Corporal Smedley survived Andersonville

Pvt. Joseph Kawell, Co. E, 18th Pennsylvania Cavalry.
Captured Jan. 12, 1864 at Allis Ford, Va., sent to Richmond
and later Andersonville. Admitted to hospital Aug. 9, 1864
and died of Scorbutus on the same date. Buried in
Grave #5145. Courtesy of Lee Joyner Collection.

and like many others was transferred out in September to a Florence, South Carolina prison. On the night of November 16th, afflicted with chronic diarrhea and dysentery he passed away there. A comrade, one Richard Dobbins of the 17th Iowa Infantry wrote; "(I) secured his Bible, diary, a small book in which he kept photographs of his family, and a few little tools with which he used to while away the time in making bone rings & c.; all of which, with the watch, according to my promise, I have succeeded in delivering to his father. [6]

Weeks and even months of imprisonment took its toll on the densely packed compound. The death rate steadily increased as emaciated and sick men traded rumors of exchange and hope. George G. Russell, a Massachusetts soldier, was captured at the Wilderness in May, 1864. After being ushered into the compound, he and his comrades were "...immediately surrounded by the inmates eager for news. ...nor was

I in no wise prepared for the sights which now met my view. I was filled with horror and my mental comment was, 'Have I come to this?' Strange skeleton men in tattered, faded blue...so obscured with dirt were their habiliments, crowded around us. Their faces were so begrimed with pitch pine smoke and dirt that for awhile we could not discover whether they were Negroes or white men. The air...seemed putrid. Offal and filth covered the ground...." Charles Fosdick of the 5th Iowa Infantry entered the stockade in February, 1864. By May, his was a tattered lot. "Our clothing was giving out until many were nearly nude. My faithtul old army shoes had become things of the past, my shirt dropped off a piece at a time until it disappeared, my hat was worn out...my blouse sleeves were worn off to the shoulder and my pants worn off to the knees.

In reality, the prison was a vast open aired city, beset by overpopulation, starvation and disease. Like a city it had streets, albeit dirt, and avenues where commerce thrived. Here could also be heard the inticing call of the gambling barker. Games of chance such as chuck a luck and faro did a brisk business. Crude shelters and tents housed barber shops where one could get his lice infested hair and or beard cut for money, food or other items of value. Some ran small restaurants, offering to cook rations for those who had no implements. The cost was usually a portion of the ration. Jewelers fashioned ornate objects from brass tintype mats and discarded objects of metal, wood and bone. Tailors patched nearly threadbare clothing for something extra to eat. Soldiers fortunate enough to have fresh water from a newly dug well sold drinks to their thirsty comrades. Corn beer was made in the prison in wooden barrels placed out in the sun for several days containing a mixture of cornmeal and water. This fermented concoction was sampled by many a prisoner, believing it to have antiscorbutic qualities. To be sure, these varying enterprises gave strength and hope to many who would have otherwise perished.

Lieutenant G.E. Sabre of the 2nd Rhode Island Cavalry, himself an Andersonville prisoner, wrote of commercial enterprise in Andersonville; "Some...prisoners, inclined to speculations, who had a little surplus meal...baked it into sap-jacks and biscuits. These they would offer for sale. Those who had money, ...having...a taste for this agreeable transformation of ground corn, purchased liberally...." [7] Other capitalists traded with the guards when officers were absent. Brass uniform buttons from prisoners uniforms, carved and other handmade items were given the sentries in exchange for tobacco, yams, turnips, and, at times, Confederate newspapers. Sabre continued: "Frequently a number of prisoners, allowed to go outside with the working parties, bought from the farmers in the neighborhood. This resulted in a competition of prices, as the latter were able to sell at a much lower price than the sutler" [8] (the sutler was a Confederate merchant who operated within the compound).

Before leaving Andersonville, Sabre gave an overview of the Andersonville economy. "By the time I was transferred from Camp Sumter, Market Street (the chief avenue of the rison which ran across the width of the compound from the North Gate to the far wall) had grown into a business mart of considerable respectability. Booths and tables were erected, and a display of eatables spread out quite flattering to the fertility of Southwestern Ga. The only obstacle...was the exceedingly limited supply of 'legal tender.' Even to those who had no funds, the markets were a source of benefit, in the amusement they afforded, and the relief of the mind from the wearying sameness of everyday life." [9]

Pvt. William H. Dutton, Co. K, 16th Connecticut Volunteer Infantry. Captured April 24, 1864 at Plymouth, N.C. One of the "Plymouth Pilgrims" sent to Andersonville. Died September 14, 1864 of dysentery. Buried in Grave #8769. Courtesy of the Lee Joyner Collection, George S. Whiteley, IV, photographer.

The prospect of escape rested on the minds of a number of prisoners. Andersonville, it will be remembered, was far removed from federal lines and escaping prisoners were often tracked by hounds kept at the post for that specific purpose. Unsuccessful escapees were sometimes clasped into wooden stocks or became part of a prison chain gang, carrying or dragging a heavy cannonball when walking. Prisoners at times eluded guards on work details outside the compound. Wood gathering and burial details were popular among the inmates, not just for the escape opportunities they provided, but for the fresh air, exercise and often times better rations that were provided.

The most popular method of escape usually associated with Andersonville was "tunneling." Having to a limited degree been issued shovels and other implements by the authorities for the purpose of digging wells, the prisoners also used sharpened sticks, railroad spikes, canteen halves, pocket knives and eating utensils to dig in the Georgia earth. Secrecy regarding such a venture was imperative and tunnel traitors who reported the diggings to the guards were dealt with severely by their peers. The whole operation of tunneling was a risky venture indeed, not only because of the chance of being found out, but because of the danger of cave-ins. A number of would-be-escapees were buried alive when the excavations collapsed. Regardless of the risks involved, a number of men were successful in obtaining their freedom from tunneling. William N. Tyler served in Company 1, 9th Illinois Cavalry and Company B, 95th Illinois Infantry. He described the tunnel he and his comrades dug and their successful escape from Andersonville. "We finally concluded to start in one of our wells which we had dug about sixty feet without getting water. This well was about seventy-five feet from the stockade; so we went down about eighteen feet and commenced digging a tunnel in under the stockade . Night after night we worked and threw the dirt into the well until we filled it to the place started from. Then we handed the dirt up in part of a blanket, and carried it down and threw it in the mire. This all had to be done at night, for the rebel guards were on the watch, and the least thing that looked suspicious was investigated immediately. So we labored away, night after night, till we were sure we had passed the stockade and then commenced to dig up toward the surface."[10] Tyler and his twelve comrades did escape, but the group he was with was recaptured a few days after the escape and put back in the stockade. It is not known what happened to the other escapees.

For many, Andersonville was the final bivouac. Existing prison diaries and authentic accounts of prison life are filled with scenes of the dead and dying. Warren Lee Goss, of the 2nd Massachusetts Heavy Artillery and himself a prisoner at Andersonville wrote, "During July (1864) one could scarcely step without seeing some poor victim in his last agonies. The piteous tones of entreaty, the famine-stricken look of these men, their bones in some cases worn through their flesh, were enough to excite pity and compassion in hearts of stone." [11] Goss and his fellow prisoners did what they could to lessen the sufferings of their dying comrades, but after a while many prisoners became nearly hardened to the daily scenes of soldiers breathing their last breath.

Although Andersonville will forever be linked to misery and death, in truth, men died by the thousands in prisons on both sides. Elmira, Johnson's Island and Camp Douglas were names equally despised among Southern soldiers and their families. Widows, orphans and relatives on both sides of the Mason-Dixon Line experienced the pain and loss of losing loved ones far away from home. Be they Northern or Southern, the civil war prisoners were all Americans and each fought and served a cause in which he believed.

Interior view of the stockade.
Courtesy of the National Archives.

Replica of Stockade Wall, 1995.

NOTES

1.   *War Record of Edward T Abbott* - (typescript of war time diary, ca. 1933) - by Edward T. Abbott, Co. H, 20th Conn. Vol. Inf. Reg't. - author's collection.

2.   *The American Heritage Collection of Civil War Art* - Stephen W. Sears, Editor. McGraw-Hill, New York, New York, 1974.

3.   *A Casualty At Gettysburg and Andersonville - Selections From The Civil War Diary of Private Austin A. Carr of the 82nd N.Y. Infantry* - ed. by David G. Martin - Longstreet House, Hightower, NJ, 1990.

4.   [Unpublished Manuscript] - "Statement of Private Joseph Morris, Company G, 23rd Kentucky Vol. Inf. Reg't as told to an officer of the New York State Militia, May 17, 1865" - author's collection.

5.   *Narrative of Amos E. Stearns A Prisoner at Andersonville* , Amos E. Stearns,1886.

6.   *Life in Southern Prisons From the Diary of Corporal Charles Smedley of Company G, 90th Regiment Penn. Volunteers* , The Ladies' and Gentlemen's Fulton Aid Society, 1865.

7.   *Reminiscences of Andersonville Prison - A Paper Read by Comrade Geo. G. Russell, Before Post 34, G.A.R.- Tuesday Evening June 22*, Salem, Mass., 1886.

8.   *Five Hundred Days in Rebel Prisons* , by Charles Fosdick, 1887.

9.   *Nineteen Months A Prisoner of War* , by Lt. G.E. Sabre, 2nd Rhode Island Cavalry, New York, The American News Company, 1865.

10.   *The Dispatch Carrier and Memoirs of Andersonville Prison* , by Comrade Wm. N. Tyler, Port Byron "Globe" Print, Port Byron, Ill., 1892.

11.   *The Soldiers Story of His Captivity at Andersonville, Belle Isle and other Rebel Prisons*, Warren Lee Goss, Boston, Lee and Shepard Publishers, 1866.

The Providence Springs Memorial.
Erected by the Women's Memorial
Association of the Grand Army of the Republic.

Mauriel Joslyn

Chapter Eight

The U. S. Policy of Retaliation on Confederate Prisoners of War

---

Mauriel Joslyn, a native of Manchester, Georgia, was educated at Mary Washington College in Fredericksburg, Virginia, and has written articles for *Gettysburg Magazine, Georgia Journal,* and *Ancestry.* Joslyn is a descendant of a Confederate prisoner of war and has written a book about the Immortal Six-Hundred (Confederate officers used as human shields against artillery by the Federals) which will soon be released by White Mane Publishing.

In 1864, a meeting occurred in Geneva, Switzerland, spurred by the benevolence of Florence Nightingale. It was an international effort to define the limits on treatment of wounded soldiers, war-torn civilians, and prisoners of war. Its mission was to enforce a civilized and humane set of standards for the innocent victims whose only wrong was to fight for their country. This meeting was the foundation for the Geneva Convention which, in modern times, has become synonymous with prisoner of war—a code of ethics that warring nations are expected to comply with. The United States chose not to participate in this humanitarian mission.

At the time this enlightened document was being conceived, the United States was at war, an internal conflict caused by a clash of cultures, imperialism, and a fight for rights guaranteed by the Constitution. However, it was not simply preoccupation with a war which kept the United States from the agreement in Geneva. In its own Congress a debate was raging which was in direct opposition to the Convention's aims. The policy of Retaliation on Prisoners of War was strongly urged to be officially adopted as law.

Retaliation was not a new word in the history of the laws of war. Regarding prisoners it had been used by General George Washington during the American Revolution to terminate mistreatment by the British of captured American soldiers, whom the British saw as "rebels and traitors" instead of legitimately fighting for a recognized country. Washington used it regrettably, and when the war was over, in 1785 a provision was signed between the United States and Prussia to end mistreatment of prisoners of war so that cruelty was not needed to enforce the laws.

The subsequent wars in which the United States was engaged saw good treatment by both sides. The War of 1812 and the Mexican War hold admirable records for the treatment of prisoners of war.

What happened to those standards by 1864? Three years earlier, the North had instigated an act of retaliation, setting a course that would wind and twist around the excuses for subsequent acts as the war's motives and methods changed. The first wave in an ocean of incidents occurred in June 1861, involving Confederate Naval personnel.

Immediately following the firing on Fort Sumter, President Jefferson Davis called for the arming of private vessels to raise a Confederate Navy. Privateering had been declared illegal by some nations who signed the Declaration of Paris in 1856. However, the United States had not signed the Declaration. When the *CSS Savannah* was captured by the *USS Perry* near Charleston, South Carolina on June 3, 1861,

Lincoln had no grounds to prosecute the crew. Six weeks prior to the outfitting of the *Savannah,* the Federal government had carefully concealed the fact of commissioning its own privateering vessel, the *Quaker City.*[1]

Still, the Confederate sailors were declared pirates, and after being chained in pairs and paraded before an angry populace to suffer taunts and jeers, were confined in the infamous New York jail known as the Tombs. The conditions were in direct violation to the laws of war regarding captives. After three weeks of being held as common criminals, the men were brought to trial, indicted on charges of piracy, and sentenced to be hanged for privateering.

Confederate President Jefferson Davis sought justice for the men. He sent Colonel Thomas H. Taylor with a message for Abraham Lincoln promising like treatment for captives. "Painful as will be the necessity, the Government will deal out to the prisoners held by it the same treatment and the same fate as shall be experienced by those captured on the *Savannah,'* he warned, "to secure the abandonment of a practice so unknown to the warfare of civilized man, and so barbarous as to disgrace the nation which shall be guilty of inaugurating it." No response was ever received from Lincoln. [2]

Andersonville National Cemetery

The trial drew outrage from Europe, the Earl of Derby and other members of the English Parliament declaring "If one thing was clearer than another it was that privateering was not piracy," and it "would be an act of barbarity which would produce an outcry throughout the civilized world," to prosecute it as such. Even many citizens of the North could not understand why these sailors should be treated as pirates while Confederate soldiers taken in land battles were considered prisoners of war. The inconsistency in policy would escalate. [3]

The trial continued, commencing in October despite the protests from abroad and at home. On November 1, 1861 a mistrial was declared, and a second trial dropped when Davis announced that fourteen captured Union soldiers would be tried under the same rules applied by the Union. A deluge of letters from family and friends to the U.S. Government prevented any action on the part of the Confederate government, and the Union sailors were never in danger. However, it wasn't until the summer of 1862 that the Confederate sailors from *Savannah* were released, broken both in health and finances.

The summer of 1862 saw the war turn bloody, with thousands of troops involved. The consequences were an accumulation of prisoners for both sides, and some agreement had to be enforced. The Lincoln Administration announced early on that the Southern states were "in rebellion," and any prisoners taken would be looked upon as traitors. If the government agreed to treat Confederate soldiers as lawful prisoners of war, it would equal a recognition of the South as a legitimate nation. Because of this interpretation, innocent soldiers became pawns in a game of politics.

Finally, Congress forced Lincoln to yield to negotiations for a prisoner exchange cartel. Union General John Dix met with Confederate General Daniel H. Hill, and the Dix-Hill Cartel emerged on July 22, 1862, releasing the captives of both sides by an even exchange according to rank. For a year, the cartel was effective, despite some infringements by Northern authorities, chiefly in the person of Secretary of War Edwin M. Stanton, who like Lincoln, resented acknowledgement of the South as a belligerent power. The success of the document lay in the agents of exchange appointed by each side, Colonel Robert Ould for the Confederacy and Major John Mulford for the Union, both of whom genuinely cared only to achieve the best for the prisoners whose lives their decisions affected. [4]

This harmony was to be short-lived. A new factor arose concerning Northern soldiers. The prisoners, once exchanged, rarely returned to their regiments. Their one year enlistments were up, few reinlisted, and the army was not getting the full benefit of the returned men. On the contrary, the Southern soldiers returned to their ranks almost to a man. This difference in patriotic duty led to doubts on the part of the Lincoln Administration. Secretary of War Stanton declared "There is reason to fear, that many voluntarily surrender for the sake of getting home."[5]

With this as an incentive, exchange of commissioned officers was cancelled by Stanton in December 1862, making the cartel equivalents impossible to fill. To complicate matters a new Union commissioner of prisoner exchange was appointed in the person of Major General Ethan Allen Hitchcock, an abrasive and inflexible proponent of abolishing exchange. His philosophy on alleviating the suffering of prisoners was to defeat the Confederate Army. Special exchanges continued under the efforts of Ould and Mulford, but the prisons began to swell in numbers after the Battle of Fredericksburg.

The threats and reports of retaliation for petty offenses continued to surface sporadically at various prisons. An example of one such instance occurred in December 1862, involving two Confederate officers of Calhoun and Jackson Counties in Northwestern Virginia. Captain Daniel Dusky and Lieutenant Jacob Varner organized a militia group to repel Federal troops from Ripley in Jackson County. Overwhelmed by superior numbers, they agreed to surrender to Federal authorities if they would receive proper treatment as prisoners of war. Receiving this promise, they surrendered, but were immediately sent to the penitentiary at Wheeling, indicted, tried, convicted, and sentenced to hard labor for four years as felons—all contrary to the proper treatment due prisoners of war.

Governor John Letcher of Virginia protested this illegal treatment of "officers, soldiers, and citizens of Virginia" by the invading Federal army. He wrote President Abraham Lincoln on January 2, 1863, "I respectfully ask that some arangement should be made for the proper exchange of the prisoners named and some agreement be entered into for the exchange of all state prisoners hereafter." He went on to suggest that if the officers were not released, the Confederate authorities would "unflinchingly retaliate" for any improper, unusual or harsh treatment practiced upon soldiers or citizens of his state. "The sin of its commencement shall rest upon the Government of the United States," concludes the letter.

Letcher was supported by President Davis in the matter of retaliation, but when brought before the Confederate Congress later that month, the decision to use retaliation was strongly opposed.

As for the two Confederate officers, they were placed on a chain gang. The correspondence continued back and forth, Federal authorities refusing to exchange the men. Finally two Union officers, Captain

William Gramm and Lieutenant Isaac A. Wade, were captured and confined in Richmond. Since the United States would not exchange Varner and Dusky, Gramm and Wade were denied exchange also. In double retaliation for this act, Governor Francis H. Peirpont, put in power in Western Virginia by Union authorities, sent the two Confederate prisoners to Albany prison, where they were still confined on May 14, 1863, at hard labor.

The Union agent of exchange, Lieutenant-Colonel William H. Ludlow questioned the validity of this action. In a letter to Colonel William Hoffman, the U.S. Commissary-General of Prisoners, he wrote, "I hope I am correct in the opinion that Governor Peirpont has no authority whatever over military captures and that some restriction may be promptly placed on this system of retaliation which seems to be going on without the knowledge or consent of the Secretary of War." His opinion was upheld by the Judge-Advocate General's office in a report to Secretary of War Edwin M. Stanton on June 5, 1863, stating "The proceedings of Governor Peirpont in seizing and confining suspected rebels in his vicinity, placing them in a chain gang and holding them at hard labor until certain civilians and officers of West Virginia are released and exchanged by the enemy is certainly an interference with the disposition and treatment of prisoners of war which must needs be very embarrassing....and that by taking it upon himself to hold rebel prisoners for exchange for Union men he necessarily interferes with the formal arrangements made by the proper officers for the same purpose."[6] Incidents of this same degree were going on at every Union prison, involving hundreds of cases.

In 1863, the reasonably calm sea of diplomacy on prisoner of war affairs became rough, as the storm of the war grew in intensity. In January, Lincoln issued the Emancipation Proclamation, announcing that slaves in Southern states were freed, despite the fact that he had no authority in that region. The document forced the question on the status of black troops taken in battle. The South had adopted the policy that any former slave captured in battle was to be returned to his master as recovered property. In answer the North, having adopted the goal of freeing the slaves, declared any slave who had joined the Union Army free from the designation as property, and entitled to treatment as a regular prisoner of war.

The issue of recovered slaves being entitled to equal treatment as white soldiers was not to be compromised by the Confederate Congress. Union authorities made this new question the pivot on which the whole exchange question turned. It became an unpopular issue in the North, where demands for exchange were a growing concern. Author and editor Walt Whitman wrote a letter to the New York Times on December 27, 1864, which spoke for the feelings of many Northern citizens. He stated in regard to the question of black troops that Stanton and Butler had "taken [their] stand on the exchange of all black soldiers, has persisted in it without regard to consequences, and has made the whole of the large and complicated question of general exchange turn upon that one item alone, while it is but a drop in the bucket...In my opinion, the anguish and death of these ten to fifteen thousand American young men, with all the added and incalculable sorrow, long drawn out, amid families at home, rests mainly upon the heads of members of our own Government."

At this stalemate a new figure entered the prisoner of war drama. Lincoln was walking a fine line to justify his stance on black soldiers, and he knew it. He must manipulate the laws of war to support his policy, and he found his man in Francis Lieber, a law professor who had emigrated from Germany in the 1840s. Lieber was known for his lectures on the U.S. Constitution and strong principles upholding individual rights .[7]

The result of his counsel was General Orders No. 100, better known as the Lieber Code. It is recognized as the first written document to acknowledge that prisoners of war are to be guaranteed the same treatment as their captors concerning food, shelter, and conditions. It also stipulates that they are not to be confined in a place of danger. Though the Confederacy had no written document, the Confederate Congress had passed the same stipulations regarding prisoners in its first session on May 21, 1861. As for retaliation, article 28 of the Code states: "Retaliation will therefore never be resorted to as a measure of mere revenge but only as a means of protective retribution and moreover cautiously and unavoidably...it shall only be resorted to after careful inquiry into the real occurence and the character of the misdeeds that may demand retribution." [8]

The campaigns during 1863 depleted the ranks of both armies in the form of prisoners and death. Chancellorsville, Vicksburg and Port Hudson, and Gettysburg racked up a grisly score measured knee deep in blood. When the numbers were figured, the dead alone exceeded 12,600 and the prisoners swelled the cells to overcrowding in both North and South. More than ever, lives depended on prisoner exchange to relieve the drain on supplies and army strength. In the face of this emergency, U.S. Secretary of War Stanton callously issued General Orders No. 207 on July 3, 1863. It declared all paroles after this date worthless. Exchange was officially cancelled.

With the refusal on the part of the North to continue exchanging prisoners of war in the summer of 1863, the number of Southern soldiers in Federal prisons had grown to over 35,700. Despite this awesome number, the North had the resources to care for the men.

Union widow visits the grave of her husband at
the Andersonville National Cemetery. Photographer and
date unidentified. Courtesy of the National Park Service.

Factories turned out army blankets, and cheap, gray uniform-style clothing. The well organized Medical Department of the U.S. Army was gorged with medicine, bandages, tents and linens. Yet the conditions at Northern prisons were horrible and little effort was expended to improve the sanitary and nutritional needs. The attitude of the North was comparable to "ethnic cleansing," whereby one culture sets out to exterminate another. Many Northerners truly wanted to inflict this upon the South, but ironically the rhetoric spewed out by the U.S. Government was the desire to restore Southerners as citizens of the Union. With this frame of mind, the attitude toward captives regressed to Barbaric Times.

In November 1863, Captain William Sydney Winder arrived in the sleepy South Georgia town of Anderson. He was sent from Richmond by his father Confederate General John Henry Winder, to find a new location for a prisoner of war camp. The new facility would be far removed from the battle front in Virginia, and alleviate the overcrowding and poor conditions of the Richmond prisons. Little did the small hamlet on the only railroad line south from Macon know it would become infamous as Andersonville.

The prison was called Camp Sumter, a stockade type tent city comprising seventeen acres. When the first inmates arrived on February 27, 1864, Lieutenant James Madison Page of the 6th Michigan Cavalry was one of the first to walk through the south gate. The site appealed to him, as it had to Captain Winder. "I don't believe a better choice could have been made. The place was healthful and salubrious and the water was good."[9]

In April 1864, a new commissioner of prisoner exchange for the North was appointed. Major General Benjamin "Beast" Butler examined the statistics and declared the Union the winner in captives. He pleaded for the reinstatement of exchange. Even with the equivalents of the cartel filled, the North would still hold 13,000 Confederate soldiers as the balance, and as a bargaining chip. Though Butler had been declared an outlaw in the South, Robert Ould convinced President Davis and the Confederate Congress to put old feelings aside for the good of the army, and accept Butler as a hope for reinstating exchange. Favorable negotiations were resumed, but once again fate stepped in.

On March 12, 1864 Major General Ulysses S. Grant assumed command of the Union Army. Butler was still in favor of exchange, realizing it was to the Union's benefit. There were more Southern soldiers in Northern prisons than vice versa. He also recognized the true reason for the suffering at Andersonville by August 1864. Supply lines from Atlanta had been cut by Sherman, preventing any shipments to reach the prison, including food. Grant was threatening Richmond, and the Confederates felt compelled to ship Union prisoners South, concentrating them at one point. The blockade confiscated all medicines as contraband, preventing any treatment for disease to be given to not only Confederate soldiers, but Union prisoners as well.

Grant, however, stated that no exchange would be allowed as a military advantage. "It is preferable to feed prisoners rather than fight soldiers," he said. His argument was founded on the fact that Union soldiers, when exchanged, went home because their one year enlistments were up. On the other hand, the Confederates returned to the ranks. It was simply a case of a difference in patriotic duty—not the physical condition of Northern soldiers who had been in captivity.

Grant's costly attacks on Lee at Cold Harbor and Petersburg were seen as murder by the citizens in the North, who began to question whether the war was worth the lives. McClellan was running for President on a Peace platform, and the election was only months away. A war weary nation, tired of defeat after defeat, was wandering away from supporting its politicians. Something had to be done to win Northern favor and justify the price paid in blood.

Often soldiers become prisoners by being in the wrong place at the wrong time, perhaps through an over-enthusiastic act of bravery. Sometimes they remain prisoners through their own government policy —when an ideology is considered more important than an act of humanity. To take the pressure off Lincoln and put it on the South, prisoners of war were used as an emotional incitement of anger against the Confederacy. The actions of Stanton and Grant are an example of a nation putting itself above the law—their "cause" became more highly valued than the interests of humanity itself.

The Southern prisons were overcrowded and suffered from a lack of resources to care for Union prisoners. The shortage of necessities was caused by a new situation in warfare. The concept of "total war" introduced upon the South by Sherman destroyed the fabric of society and broke down the supply and transportation lines of the Confederate Government and Army. Government officials had pleaded to reinstate exchange as early as September 1863, in order to empty prisons like Libby and Belle Isle in Richmond. The North refused, Secretary of War Edwin N. Stanton vascillating his position on the topic depending on what interpretation worked best in favor of Union interests.

With the campaigns by Grant against Richmond, the prison at Camp Sumter, Georgia filled quickly. Its new commander, Captain Henry

Wirz arrived in April, and set about immediately to expand the facilities, but supplies became unobtainable. By August 32,000 men were crowded on seventeen acres, with not enough water, food or medical supplies. Despite the attempts by Confederate surgeons to obtain vegetables and medicine, the naval blockade, and destruction of crops by Sherman's troops rendered any relief impossible. At Andersonville over 10,000 men had died by September 1864. The solution was exchange, or moving the prisoners. In a stopgap measure to end the death toll, many were shipped to Charleston and Savannah, while a new facility was constructed at Columbia, South Carolina. This broke up Camp Sumter, and by November, it was empty.

Many soldiers took the opportunity to make their escape while being moved. They brought back tales of suffering and death to comrades and friends. No doubt they had suffered. No doubt the Confederate authorities had done all they could to prevent it.

The Union set up an impossible situation for the Confederate Government, both militarily and logistically, then screamed "Foul!" The citizens of the North were manipulated into thinking the South was withholding food and supplies from Union prisoners on purpose, while the South continued to plead for exchange. But the plea fell on deaf ears. The people of the North only heard what their leaders told them. Finally 13,000 Union prisoners were sent North without receiving any Confederate soldiers in exchange, simply as an act of humanity on the part of the Confederate Government. [10]

However, the citizens of the North were fed stories of atrocities and mistreatment, and believing these rumors, sought retribution against the captives in their midst. On December 20, 1864, House Resolution No. 96 was introduced in the United States Congress. Senator Henry Smith Lane, a rabid proponent of retaliation, introduced the bill to the 38th U.S. Congress on December 20, 1864 which became known as the Lane Resolution. It promoted behavior which was strictly in violation of the laws of war as well as the United States Government's own document, the Lieber Code.

The preamble read:

> Rebel prisoners in our hands are to be subjected to a treatment finding its parallels only in the conduct of savage tribes and resulting in the death of multitudes by the slow but designed process of starvation and by mortal diseases occasioned by insufficient and unhealthy food and wanton exposure to their persons to the inclemency of the weather. [11]

The argument for retaliation was passionately sold on the floor of Congress by Senators Lane, Benjamin F. Wade of Ohio, and Morton Smith Wilkinson of Minnesota. They promised it would achieve the goal of forcing the Confederacy to supply Union prisoners with food and appropriate shelter and clothing. Most knew better. One of Lincoln's own generals, Dan Sickles, wrote the president that retaliation would do no good. "The enemy are reported to be without the means to supply clothing, medicines, and other medical supplies even to their own troops," he wrote on August 10, 1864. Lincoln did nothing. Other more moderate Senators, Hendricks of Indiana and Charles Sumner of Massachusetts denounced such cruelty based on "vague rumor" and "uncertain report." Besides, it was against the laws of nations governing captives.

While Congress was still only debating it, retaliation was enforced by the North, at the discretion of commandants and field commanders. When a report was received that the only rations available at Andersonville and Salisbury were cornmeal and molasses, the Confederate soldiers in Northern prisons were denied available food, and put on cornmeal and pickles. When it was heard that supplies of blankets and winter clothing could not be delivered to the prisons in the South because of military operations by the North, or destroyed rail lines, these same articles were taken away from Southerners—whose own families had sent them in many cases—purely as an act of retribution. The winter in the North without blankets was impossible to survive, and many innocent men froze to death. Great Britain was aware of the treatment, and a ship loaded with supplies for 8,000 Southern soldiers in Northern prisons was not allowed to be landed. Even though no good was gained by it, the deadly policy of retaliation continued to be enforced.

One particular group of Confederate officer prisoners were singled out and set aside specifically for a special purpose. These men would become the measure for how much abuse to mete out. First used as human shields under friendly fire in Charleston Harbor, they became known as the Immortal Six Hundred. For forty-five days they survived shelling under the guns of Fort Moultrie and the batteries around Charleston. Then they were taken to Fort Pulaski, Georgia and Hilton Head, South Carolina where they wintered on retaliation rations of cornmeal and pickles, suffering from frostbite and cold with no blankets. Some walked the floor all night to keep from freezing to death. Forty four men starved to death before they were released from Fort Delaware after the war in the summer months of 1865. The surviving officers filed a war claims case in 1914 that would have been won under the Geneva Convention laws at Nuremberg in 1945-49. However they lost their case because they could not "prove" that Secretary of War Edwin M. Stanton ordered the treatment. [12]

The Retaliation Resolution passed in Congress on January 31, 1865 by a vote of 24 to 16. The chivalry and civilized treatment of prisoners of war which originated in Christian Western Civilization during the 1400s became non-existent in the winter of 1864-65. It was almost immediately made obsolete and dropped when prisoner of war exchange was resumed in late February. Only the collapse of the Confederacy and end of the war curtailed the Lane Resolution. Legal murder was accepted by the victors, while the defeated South was tried and convicted of mistreatment, and scapegoat Captain Henry Wirz paid with his life for the crime of being on the losing side.

Edward Wellington Boate was a soldier in the 42nd New York Infantry, and a prisoner at Andersonville in 1864. He wrote of his experiences in the New York Times shortly after the war, and commented on whom he held responsible for Andersonville's legacy.

"You rulers who make the charge that the rebels intentionally killed off our men, when I can honestly swear they were doing everything in their power to sustain us, do not lay this flattering unction to your souls. You abandoned your brave men in the hour of their cruelest need. They fought for the Union, and you reached no hand out to save the old faithful, loyal, and devoted servants of the country. You may try to shift the blame from your own shoulders, but posterity will saddle the responsibility where it justly belongs." [13]

The atrocities committed by the North against prisoners of war fill the pages of the Official Records of the War of the Rebellion, but are carefully left out of most "unbiased" accounts. Perhaps in the twentieth century, or the twenty-first, with reports of the abandonment of its own soldiers in the Second World War and Vietnam, the truth will be released in regard to the United States Government's actions of the past.

NOTES

1.   *Pirates or Patriots?* Charles Rice. *America's Civil War,* September 1994.

2.   Ibid.

3.   Ibid.

4.   *Immortal Captives: The Story of 600 Confederate Officers and the U.S. Policy of Retaliation.* Mauriel Phillips Joslyn, White Mane Press 1995.

5.   *Civil War Prisons: A Study in War Psychology,* William B. Hesseltine, New York 1930. p. 77.

6.   *Official Records of the War of the Rebellion.* Series II vol. 5, p. 147,148,222,227,266,267,350,6ll-13.

7.   *Prisoners of War: A Study in the Development of International Law.* William E.S. Flory, Washington, DC., 1942. P. 18-19.

8.   *Official Records,* Series II vol. 5, General Order No. 100 p. 671-73.

9.   *The True Story of Andersonville and Other Military Prisons of the South in 1864.* James Madison Page, New York 1908. p. 61.

10.   *Andersonville and Other War Prisons.* Jefferson Davis, New York 1890.

11.   *Congressional Globe, Senate Rept. 142, Pt. 3 38th Congress,* 2nd Session. p. 268.

12.   *Immortal Captives.*

13.   *Southern Historical Society Papers,* vol. 10, 1886. p. 32.

Wayne Dobson

Chapter Nine

All Were Prisoners There

John Wayne Dobson, a historical researcher living in Macon, Georgia, has written articles for *Middle Georgia Magazine,* the *Confederate Veteran,* the *Macon Telegraph,* the *Warner Robins Daily Sun,* and other local publications. Dobson is the descendant of an Andersonville guard, Corporal William L. Dobson, and served as a reenactor during the 1994 filming of the Turner television movie *Andersonville.* This article first appeared in *Middle Georgia Magazine* and now includes the names of a number of men who served as prison guards at Camp Sumter.

About midnight the train stopped, and we were ordered off...Five hundred weary men moved along slowly through double lines of guards. Five hundred men marched silently towards the gates that shut out life and hope for most of them forever. A quarter of a mile from the railroad, we came to a massive palisade of great squared logs standing upright in the ground. The fires blazed and showed us a section of these, and two massive gates, with heavy iron bolts and hinges. They swung open as we stood there and we passed through it into the space beyond. We were in Andersonville."

-John McElroy, Co. L. 16th Illinois Cavalry

"We parted with our Alabama guards early in April. It was a disappointment to us, for we had found friends among them, real friends who shared with us their scant allowance. Others who had nothing 'gave all they had—a tear.'"

Such was the recollection of Lt. James Madison Page, 6th Michigan Cavalry, of his prison guards at Camp Sumter, better known as Andersonville. Could these same men be the monsters spoken of at the post-war trial of Capt. Henry Wirz, the commander of that notorious place, and the only man tried and executed for war crimes committed during the war between the states?

When Capt. William Sidney Winder arrived in Sumter County, Georgia, from Virginia, it was a cold November day in 1863. He was the son of Gen. John Henry Winder, Confederate Commissary General of Prisoners. His mission—to find a new prison site far from the battlefront in Virginia. Sumter County was remote, the soil and resources good, and most importantly, could provide a respite for Union prisoners of war from the overcrowded conditions at Libby and Belle Isle in Richmond. The initial plans were for a temporary stockade, enclosing about seventeen acres, with the intention of adding barracks later.

Lt. James Madison Page of the 6th Michigan Cavalry was glad to leave the suffocating boxcar he had ridden in for a week and disembarked with about a thousand other men for a pilgrimage never expected when they enlisted two years earlier. Leaving the train, the first of the eventual 32,899 men to be confined at Andersonville, were marched to the unfinished pine log stockade. One foot thick and set in a trench five feet deep, the logs formed a wall fifteen feet high. The smell of pine rosin was strong, as axes were at work that very moment cutting timber to complete the wall. Around the top, spaced thirty-five feet apart stood sentry boxes, manned by veteran troops from the 25th Alabama "who knew how to treat prisoners." This regiment was one of many furnished as guards during their temporary absence from the death and destruction of the front lines, and Lee's Army.

All accounts of the war, from men of both sides, consistently claim that guards who had seen action on the battlefield were respectful and humane. Courage loves courage, and a sympathy existed between these soldiers, many of whom had fought each other hand to hand on the field of honor. It was the militia troops, the "Home Guard," who were to be feared. Having never met the enemy on the field, these green troops were often nervous and lacked confidence, making them quick to shoot first and ask questions later. Some harbored a hatred of the enemy for the shortages imposed by the Union blockade, and the wanton destruction of private property by Union troops.

By 1864, the southern civilian populace not only had learned a bit about their avowed enemy, the Yankees, but they had become a bit wiser of the ways of those of their own allegiance, many communities objected to having armed men in their midst. Knowing what ravages it could cause to a country simply by supporting soldiers, putting a prison in Sumter County was not a popular decision as far as the locals were concerned. The attempt had already been struck down in the Albany, Georgia area.

Capt. Winder found himself in a perplexing position. The guard detail would be but one of many problems he would encounter. The first guards to arrive were not even armed, and the total accumulation of sentinels would never be considered adequate. At one time only 300 stood watch over 7,000 captives. When the prison population peaked in August 1864, 2,300 soldiers, almost all of them raw recruits, were guarding 32,000 prisoners. The order to shoot without hesitation any man crossing the "dead-line," which existed at all prisons North and South, was a matter of vital necessity when captives so outnumbered captors.

The first militia troops designated for Andersonville were the Georgia Reserve Corps, under the command of General Howell Cobb, headquartered in Macon. The bulk of these troops were young boys and old men, all that the homefront had left. Toward the end of March 1864, Cobb received a request from Winder at Andersonville to detail troops for guard duty. He hastily organized a camp of military instruction at Camp Nelson, located at Morganton, Georgia. There the green units, whose only service to their country had consisted of drilling in the town square, achieved a measure of military organization, and then rapidly detailed to Andersonville by rail, "to see the elephant."

The first two reserve units to arrive in May 1864 relieved the veterans of the 25th Alabama Infantry, and the 46th, 47th, and 55th Georgia Infantry. These shock troops were needed in Virginia, where Grant was on "the road to Richmond," opening with the Wilderness Campaign.

"Fresh Fish." Wartime illustration
Courtesy of the National Park Service.

These reinforcements swelled the guard detail to 1,193 effectives, including a Florida battery of rifled 10-pounders and Napoleons. The guard mount consisted of 303 men per day, posted as follows: one man in each sentry box, 40 men at each gate by day, and doubled at night for extra security. The remainder were posted in a line around the stockade, fifty yards out. Even those on relief were required to remain near their posts in case of emergency. Andersonville became a prison to all concerned.

No sooner had the reserve units gotten their duty roster written, than the Confederate high command tried to force as many furloughs through as possible. It was the first week of June, and precious crops were in the field. Someone had to be spared for harvest. A desperate need for food conflicted with the same need for prison security. As many as could be spared were farmers again, at least temporarily.

One of these boys was William Lee Andrew Dodson. At age seventeen, he had left his home in the rolling, West Georgia farmland of Carroll County, and enlisted in his country's cause. In May 1864, the tall pine walls at Andersonville must have looked almost as foreboding to him and his compatriots as it did to the Union unfortunates held captive there.

The prisoners kept under the watchful eye of the Georgia Reserves included American Indians, Negroes, the representatives of several foreign countries, and men from nearly every state in the Union at that time. Despite the chasm that separated them from the Georgians, the bond of the common shortage of the three necessities of life—food, shelter, and clothing—prompted forbidden dialog and trading. The sutler was James Selman, Jr. He was allowed to sell to the prisoners who had money, although the cost of the items he sold was high. This was a reflection of the shortage of foodstuffs, but it also netted him a substantial profit. For those who had no money, trading with the guards was common, though officially forbidden. The need for outside news to give them hope, drove the prisoners to depend on the guards for any newspapers or reports from the battlefront. Although newspapers were withheld from Confederate prisoners in most Northern prisons, they were allowed at Andersonville.

The constant hope that exchange, cancelled by the North as a war measure, would be reinstated was shared by both prisoners and their keepers. Many times the rumor was spread by guards in the hope that it would discourage any determination to escape, an event feared by local civilians was well.

The dreaded "Deadline" has become an infamy at Andersonville. One incident which occurred in May, and was used in the trial of Captain Henry Wirz to incite hatred against the unfortunate commander, involved the deadline. A prisoner was shot for crossing it. An impassioned plea by a "witness" described the offender, whose name was Hubbard of the 38th Illinois regiment, as only being in the vicinity of the deadline to escape comrades who believed he had reported them for digging an escape tunnel. The story was supposed to gain the sympathy of the jury. But according to Lt. James Madison Page, this was not true.

Hubbard had lost a leg at Chickamauga, and was "an inoffensive, garrulous creature." Because of his misfortune, and almost helpless condition, he had gained the sympathy of Wirz, and received special favors from the commander. Page witnessed the scene, and acknowledged that Hubbard was being chased by fellow prisoners as described. There the similarity of the stories end. When he crossed the deadline, the guard pleaded with him to go back. Hubbard actually sat down, with his crutches across his legs, rocking back and forth while the guard went for a superior officer. Capt. Wirz attempted to make

Hubbard go back inside the enclosure, and hoping all was resolved, left the scene. The sentry continued to order Hubbard to move, when he was suddenly taunted by the prisoners as a coward for not firing. Insulted, the sentry reluctantly fired the fatal round, hitting Hubbard in the head and killing him instantly. Seeing what he had done, he then sat down his musket, and "buried his face in his hands" with remorse. It was the mob, and not the act of a lone sentry which resulted in the tragedy.

For the guards, their duty was in some ways as arduous and confining as prison was for the Union soldiers under their surveillance. Disease did not discriminate, whether the uniform be blue or gray. Though the shortage of vital items certainly hit those within the stockade the hardest, those along the watch tower also went lacking. Too few tends caused exposure and suffering to both friend and foe, while the hot summer sun took its toll in sunstroke on guards along the parapet. The mundane diet of sub-standard foods wore on the health and nerves of all, and rice often contained as much dirt as grain. Corn meal made for a monotonous diet.

Johnny Mines served at Andersonville with
Co. B of the 3rd Georgia Regiment. He surrendered
in April, 1865 on the Columbus Road in Macon Georgia.
Courtesy of Patrick G. Mines.

The combination of the horrible conditions caused by overcrowding and the threat of Sherman's forces liberating the prison caused Gen. John H. Winder to order the removal of the prisoners from Andersonville. Beginning in September 1864, they were shipped to Savannah, Charleston, and Columbia, South Carolina, places thought more secure. Indeed the conditions were much better, and none had the death toll of Andersonville. The guards were dispersed to meet the threats of Sherman's bummers, and virtually empty by the end of 1864, Andersonville passed into the pages of history.

Those who survived, both warden and captive alike, would spend the remainder of their days haunted by the memories of the sights, smells and sounds of that fatal place. The guards who died and were buried there were relocated to family plots and churchyards. They were on the losing side, and their story is overshadowed by the thousands of graves of Union dead now turned into a National Cemetery.

Many written accounts suddenly appeared in the years following the war, brimming with hatred and telling horrible examples of the cruelty and inhumane treatment at Andersonville. The guards were lumped together as a set of beastly jailors with little feeling for their charges. After reading these sensational stories designed to arouse the passions of Northerners against the defeated South, James Madison Page determined to set the story straight.

"Touching my treatment on the whole, I cannot recall a solitary instance, during the fourteen months while I was a prisoner, of being insulted, browbeaten, robbed, or maltreated in any manner by a Confederate officer or soldier," he wrote. "With all respect to my late brethren-inarms in prison life I cannot but think that to some extent they were instrumental, if they state facts, in bringing this treatment upon themselves...I know that many of them were curt and irritable in their intercourse with the guards."

Except for the honesty of men like Page, the true story of the men who are often held responsible for much of the suffering at Andersonville has gone untold. Yet they suffered the same privations, shared the same sickness, and lived on the same hopes just as their captives did, that prisoner exchange would be reinstated, the war would end, and peace would once again come to Sumter County.

Corporal William Lee Andrew Dobson was paroled in Albany, Georgia in May 1865. The following November he married the first of three wives, resumed farming and fathered thirteen children. The author is the great grandson of this former Confederate veteran and Andersonville guard.

Guards in Pigeon Roost.
Courtesy of the National Park Service.

Historians and writers have focused upon the Union prisoners at Andersonville, but what became of those men who served as Confederate guards? Were they the heartless, faceless, menacing monsters as portrayed in some accounts? Or were they simply a collection of old men and young boys serving as citizen-soldiers in the most difficult of circumstances? Researchers are hard pressed to find documentation about this aspect of the Andersonville saga. Recorded information about the Confederate military units that served at Andersonville is scarce. Nevertheless, we can obtain some information about individual soldiers who served in regular companies from the Compiled Service Records of the Federal Archives. The soldier's name, unit identification, enlistment dates, periods of service, and dates of parole are listed for some Andersonville guards. Original rosters and official papers for Georgia militia and home guards units are not easily found; they are missing in many cases. Furthermore, it appears that after the war many of the former prison guards were apprehensive about their military service under Commanders Winder and Wirz at the stockade; they thought that Federal reckoning might be brought against them. These old veterans seemed content to let this part of their military duty go unnoticed; but, bits and pieces of their experiences have filtered down to us through the generations.

One former corporal of the First Georgia Reserves at Andersonville, William L. Dobson, asked these questions until his death in 1926: "How will we be remembered after all that happened there? What will history say about us?" This former guard held strong memories about his service, and he passed down one story that is still repeated among his descendants. It seems that a group of prison guards were buying meat pies from three of the local boys in the nearby community. After the sale of the meat pies, one of the youngest of the trio broke into tears. One kindly Confederate guard took notice and began to question the young lad, "What was the matter?" To which the boy immediately replied, "My brothers won't divide the money with me, and after all...it was my puppy we used!"

William Lee Andrew Dobson served as a prison guard
at Camp Sumter with Co. F of the 1st Georgia Reserves.
Courtesy of Wayne Dobson.

Corporal Dobson was one of the lucky ones. After his service at Andersonville he returned to farming, married, raised thirteen children, and lived a long life. Others were not so fortunate: they would reap the full harvest of Federal Reconstruction, chronic disability, poverty, and early death. Johnny Mines, another member of the First Georgia Reserves, died on May 21, 1897 as an impoverished invalid; he left behind a wife, daughter, and young son. The remains of this Andersonville veteran, a "true and faithful soldier," lie in the cemetery of the Baird Baptist Church (circa 1802) in Oglethorpe County, Georgia. Some veterans, like George S. King, who enlisted in Athens, Georgia as a member of Fannin's First Georgia Reserves, Company B, were furloughed for illness prior to the end of the war. But for many, the ailments did not subside. In George King's case, he continued to suffer from bad knees, swelling feet, lung and kidney diseases, and asthma. This former guard was forced to rely on the support of his two sons; and when these sons married and moved away, Smith eventually sold his last bit of property (a yoke of oxen), and continued to seek work (as did his wife and three daughters). Some guards, like Zachariah Taylor Beckam, a seventeen year old private in Company G, were captured by Union soldiers, sent to a military prison in Macon, and were eventually paroled. Many guards were released in Albany, Georgia in May, 1865. Some of the Camp Sumter sentinels had left their post early and were declared AWOL. Many of these men had probably left to protect their families during Sherman's invasion. In many cases, these AWOL's may have had good reasons for their actions. For the most part, however, the story of the guards is best found in personal letters, diaries, veteran reminiscences, and genealogical documents.

The bodies of many of these prison guards were removed from the Confederate burial ground at Andersonville to Oak Grove Cemetery in Americus. One of the guard's descendants, Walter Scott McCleskey of Manchester, still (at age 74) reveres the stoic service of his Confederate ancestors who served in Andersonville. One of these ancestors, John Thomas Spruill, is buried under a headstone incorrectly marked "J. T. Sprace, CSA." Mr. McCleskey—and many other Georgians as well—believe that the mortality rate of the prison guards was similar to that of the Union soldiers held in captivity. In some instances sick guards were nursed by local women and sent away from the area to recover. The cemetery at Oak Grove holds the graves of 129 Confederate guards; forty-five of these are buried as unknowns. The following list contains the names of guards buried there at the Oak Grove Cemetery and is provided by Mr. McCleskey:

M. S. Donaldson, Co. H 2nd GA Res.
J.W. Johnston, Co. H 2nd GA Res.
Stephen H. Wynn, Co. F 3rd GA Res.
James V. Grant, Co. F 3rd GA Res.

Ambrose Bradford, Co. K 2nd GA Res.
W.B. Mitchell, Co. B 4th GA Res.
Samuel P. Smith, Co. G 2nd GA Res.
W.J. Stephens, Co. B 4th GA Res.
John H. Rhodes, Co. I 3rd GA Res.
Sgt. Sidney S. Sullivan, Co. K 4th GA Res.
Sgt. T. J. Johnson, Co. H 2nd GA Res.
J.T. Sprace (Spruill), Co. C 2nd GA Res.
Sgt. Thomas F. Austin, Co. C 2nd GA Res.
Able H. Ayers, Co. K 2nd GA Res.
B.I. Smith, Co. F 1st GA Res.
John Clark Crawford, Co. L 5th GA Res.
Aldred B. Gailey, Co. C 2nd GA Res.
W.C. Cathright, Co. D 1st GA Res.
Corp. W.D. Snov, Co. C 4th GA Res.
S.C. Carlton, Co. E 4th GA Res.
Samuel Avery, Co. F 1st GA Res.
Jonathan Hatcher, Co. C 2nd GA Res.
William Ballard, Co. I 2nd GA Res.
Samuel Arvey, Co. F 1st GA Res.
R.F. Bates, Co. G 4th GA Res.
W.F. Marsh, Co. B 5th GA Res.
John Pope, Co. A 1st GA Res.
J.K. Smith, Co. B 4th GA Res.
Lewis Melton, Co. A 4th GA Res.
L.L. Murray, Co. A 3rd GA Res.
John King, Co. K 3rd GA Res.
John H. Jackson, Co. H 3rd GA Res.
J.N. Brown, Co. A 1st GA Res.
B.A. Haygood, Co. B 4th GA Res.
J.W. Brown, Co. F 1st GA Res.
Charles D. Morris, Co. E 5th GA Res.
J.B. Hartley, Co. C 4th GA Res.
Benjamin L Powers, Co. F 3rd GA Res.
J.T. Glass, Co. H 3rd GA Res.
James Z. Cary, Co. A 3rd GA Res.
J.G. Fergusson, Co. G 3rd GA Res.
W.W. Giles, Co. F 1st GA Res.
Chesley Chandler, Co. B 1st GA Res.
W.T.A. Dunn, Co. A 3rd GA Res.
W.C. Gaithright, Co. D 1st GA Res.
J. McCord, Co. A 2nd GA Res.
Frank T. Ansley, Co. B 1st GA Res.

and

Dr. Samuel S. Bird C.S.A.
10-18-1830 - 11-8-1892
"Physician & Surgeon for Northern Troops at Andersonville, GA"

Gorge Sanford King (Co. B, First Ga. Reserves)
and his wife Mary. Courtesy of Patrick G. Mines.

SOURCES

Andersonville Historical Site, Edwin C. Bearss
   1970 Office of History & Historic Architecture, Washington, DC.

History of Andersonville Prison, Ovid L. Futch
   1968 University of Florida Press.

Life and Death in Rebel Prisons, Robert H. Kellogg
   1865 L. Stebbins, Hartford, Conn.

John Ransom's Diary, John L. Ransom
   1881, Paul S. Erikson, Inc., New York.

Camp Sumter, Ken Drew
   1989, U.S.A.

WALTER SCOTT MCCLESKEY
   Letters of November 18 and December 12, 1994.

SERVICE AND PENSION RECORDS OF CORP. JOHN MINES, 3RD GA. RES.

CHARLES D. JONES
   Information received December 12, 1994.

PATRICK G. MINES
   Information received December 12, 1994.

RICKY ANTHONY SMITH
   Information, graves registration: list of those buried in Oak Grove Cemetery, Americus, GA received December 12, 1994.

Diary of a Dead Man (Ira Pettit) 1862-1864, Compiled by J.P. Ray, East Acorn Press, 1981.

Official Records of the War of the Rebellion; Series II, Volume 8 Ser. #121, "Prisoners of War, Etc."

This Was Andersonville, John McElroy. Edited with an introduction by Roy Meredith. New York, Bonanza Books, 1957, page 20.

Units of the Confederate Army, by Joseph H. Crute, Jr.
   1987 Derwent Books, Midlothian, Virginia

Roster of the Confederate Soldiers of Georgia, 1861-1865. Six volumes. Compiled by Lillian Henderson, Longino & Porter, 1955-1964.

Confederate Prison Guards and their Captains.
Courtesy of the National Park Service.

Heinrich Wirz

Chapter Ten

A Response from the Wirz Family of Switzerland

A study into the Southern Perspective of Andersonville would not be complete without insight and opinion from the descendants of Captain Henry Wirz, the ill-fated commander of Camp Sumter. In this section, Colonel Heinrich Wirz, as representative of the Wirz family of Switzerland, offers response through the following documents: two letters of personal correspondence; a reprint of a memorial address delivered at Camp Douglas, Chicago, Illinois in April, 1994; and a copy of a patriotic society's resolution adopted in 1977 that expresses the sentiments of Wirz descendents living in Louisiana and Switzerland. Although brief, these selections clearly state the family's position and echo the feelings of many Southerners, past and present.

To introduce Heinrich Wirz, Mrs. Peggy Sheppard of the Andersonville Guild offers this article which she wrote for the November 2, 1993 edition of the *Americus Times Recorder* under the headline, "WIRZ DESCENDANT TO SPEAK AT ANDERSONVILLE SERVICE."

Col. Heinrich L. Wirz, Of Berne, Switzerland, an active member of the Swiss military, charter member of the European chapter of the Sons of Confederate Veterans, and greatgrandnephew of CSA Capt. Henry Hartman Wirz, keeper Of Andersonville Confederate Prison, will be principal speaker at the 17th annual Wirz Memorial Program to be held at 3 p.m. Sunday at Easterlin Square in the Village of Andersonville.

CSA Capt. Henry Wirz was the most controversial figure at the Civil War's most infamous prison. He was hung as a criminal by the North, and then honored with a monument and a posthumous medal by the South.

A native of Switzerland, Wirz came to this country 12 years before the Civil War broke out. He settled in Louisiana, joined the Fourth Louisiana infantry, was wounded on the battlefield, and was then made keeper of Andersonville Prison. The 26 1/2-acre prison stockade, built to hold no more than 10,000 prisoners, received 45,000 Union prisoners in the last 14 months of the war. The overcrowded conditions, the scarcity of food (due to the ravages of the war and the Union blockade), the contamination of the drinking water, and the poor conditions of the prisoners on arrival all contributed to the 12,912 deaths of prisoners at Andersonville. The blame was put on Wirz. He was tried for war crimes by a United States military court. He was convicted, sentenced to death, and hanged on Nov. 10, 1865. Historians and Civil War buffs have been debating the verdict of his trial ever since.

In 1909, the Georgia Division of the United Daughters of the Confederacy, believing the Wirz trial a miscarriage of justice, erected a monument to his memory in the center of the Village of Andersonville. In 1981, the Sons of the Confederate Veterans posthumously conferred on him the Confederate States of America Medal of Honor.

Among out-of-towners expected to attend the memorial program are state officials of the Sons of Confederate Veterans, the United Daughters of the Confederacy and the Confederate P.O.W. Society joint sponsors of the event. Also expected are Fred Jenny, Consul General of Switzerland in Atlanta; Mr. Glen LaForce of Ft. McPherson, historian and author of several articles about Wirz; Robert Perrin Watkins of Amite, La., great-grandson of Wirz; Perrin Johnson Watkins, William Claud Watkins, and John Dowd Watkins, great-great-grandsons of Wirz, and their spouses, all of Louisiana, and Wallis Alexandra Watkins, Desiree Wirz Watkins, Alyce Jordan Watkins and Jamie Marie Watkins, great-great-great grandchildren of Wirz, all also of Louisiana.

Colonel Heinrich Wirz, great grandnephew of Andersonville's last commander, Henry Wirz. Courtesy of Peggy Sheppard.

Heinrich L. Wirz   20 February 1995 AK/HHW/BW

Switzerland
Defense and Military Affairs Consultant and Writer. Colonel, Swiss Army (rtd) First Lieutenant Commander, Europe Camp, Sons of Confederate Veterans (SCV) European Aide-de-Camp, Military Order of the Stars and Bars (MOS&B) Member, Captain Henry Wirz Stockade, Confederate Prisoner of War Society

Captain Henry Wirz, A.A.G., C.S.A., Commandant of Camp Sumter (Andersonville)

Dear Compatriot Segars

Please excuse my delay in answering to your requests for a contribution to the book you are actually compiling, entitled "Andersonville, the Southern View." Thank you again for the copy "In Search of Confederate Ancestors: The Guide"!

I was pleased that we could discuss the matter during our telephone conversation of last Saturday, 18 February 1995. So I hurry to mail the materials which could be useful for your purpose. I omit "Mr. Louis Schade's Open Letter" and "The Trial of Major Henry Wirz - A National Disgrace" by Captain Glen W. LaForce (Confederate Veteran, Jan/Feb 1989). I met Major LaForce last August in Atlanta where we visited the Historic Oakland Cemetery, (see enclosed picture!) together with The Reverend John S. Sims. I told you about the lions in Luzern/ Lucerne, Switzerland and at the Confederate Memorial Cemetery near Higginsville, Missouri (East of Kansas City). I shall try to send pictures of both lions with a forthcoming letter to you.

I hope that in the meantime you met with Mrs. Peggy Sheppard and that she could give you some pictures and showed you the book on Captain Wirz by Jurg Weibel, which is on display in the museum at Andersonville reception center.

As enclosures you find a documentation including pictures of my great-grand-uncle and his monument at Andersonville. Please feel free to use the materials for your book or for any other activity in remembrance of my ancestor.

I could imagine that as a personal contribution to your book you could reprint the "Address of the Wirz Family" (may need some corrections of English) for the Camp Douglas Memorial Service or my letter to the editor of "Civil War Chronicles," but I do not know if it was published because I got no reaction.

If you need other informations do not hesitate to respond immediately! I shall try to answer within about ten days or give you a phone call. I wish you every success with your publications and remain

Confederately yours,

Heinrich L. Wirz

Heinrich L. Wirz   16 April 1994 AK/HHW/AU

Switzerland
Writer on Swiss Defense and Military Affairs; Colonel, Swiss Army. First Lieutenant Commander, Europe Camp, Sons of Confederate Veterans (SCV). Member of the Military Order of the Stars and Bars (MOS&B).

Camp Douglas Memorial Service: Address of the Wirz family in Switzerland

Mrs. Commandant-In-Chief of the Confederate Prisoners of War Society,
Honored members of the Sons of Confederate Veterans,
                of the United Daughters of the Confederacy,
                of the Military Order of the Stars and Bars,

Dear American friends and relatives, Ladies and Gentlemen!

In the name of the Wirz family I heartily thank you for your continuous effort in favor of the Southern prisoners during the War of Secession. "They Suffered For Us" is the motto of the Confederate Prisoners of War Society. I think all prisoners of war suffered and are still suffering for their country, for their conviction, for their comrades, for their families and even for their political and military leaders.

So suffered Captain Henry Wirz, Assistant Adjutant General, Confederate States Army, when after the War of Secession he was a prisoner of the Union Army in Washington, D.C. His military rank was sergeant when on 31 May 1862 during the battle of Seven Pines (Fair Oaks) he was severely wounded on his right arm by a rifle ball. He nearly lost use of it and was in pain for the remaining years of his life. Promoted to Captain on 12 June 1862 he was assigned as Assistant Adjutant to the staff of Brigadier General John H. Winder, Superintendent of Confederate Military Prisons, who put him on duty at Libby prison in Richmond. General Winder sent him to inspect Confederate prisons in July 1862 and then to command the Confederate prison at Tuscaloosa, Alabama. In December 1862 President Jefferson Davis sent Captain Wirz on a secret mission to the Confederate Commissioners James Mason in London and John Slidell in Paris. He returned in February of 1864 and the following April was ordered as commandant of the prison at Andersonville, Georgia, where conditions were terrible almost beyond description. In May 1865 Captain Wirz was dismissing the last prisoners when he was arrested and taken to Washington, D.C. After a long and tormenting trial he was condemned to death on 6 November 1865 and hanged in the yard of the Old Capitol Prison on 10 November 1865 at exactly 10:32 a.m. When the major commanding the execution told Captain Wirz: "I have my orders," he spoke his last words: "I know what orders are, Major - I am being hanged for obeying them."

On 6 November 1865 Captain Henry Wirz wrote a short letter to the President of the United States, Mr. Andrew Johnson. In it he said in the famous words from the Virginian patriot Patrick Henry in 1776: "Give me liberty or give me death!" You all know what he was given.

Was my great-granduncle Henry Wirz a brutal mass-murderer or an innocent scapegoat and victim of postwar hysteria after the assassination of President Abraham Lincoln? After having studied all materials collected by my father and myself, I realize that the question is still controversial. However there is a growing number of objective discussions and publications in Switzerland and in the United States and the attitude of the serious historians in both countries is definitely positive towards the former commandant of Camp Sumter, the Civil War prison at Andersonville, Georgia. So Major Glen W. LaForce, an Army Judge Advocate, wrote in his article, which appeared 1988 in "The Army Lawyer" and was reprinted 1989 in the "Confederate Veteran," that the trial of Captain Henry Wirz was worse than a mistake, worse even than a miscarriage of justice, but that it was a national disgrace: "Wirz was a scapegoat, tried in order to incriminate the Confederate leaders and to deflect criticism from Secretary of War Edwin M. Stanton."

In his last message to his attorney-at-law, Mr. Louis Frederick Schade, headed "Old Capitol Prison, Washington, D.C.," Henry Wirz wrote on 10 November 1865 -the day of his execution: "My life is demanded as an atonement. I am willing to give it, and hope that after a while, I will be judged differently from what I am now."

The Swiss descendants of Heinrich Hartmann Wirz can only hope that this will once happen. I personally have full confidence in American justice, that one day to come, the memory of Captain Henry Wirz will be vindicated by a fair trial.

My family and especially my son, Captain Thomas Heinrich Wirz, and I thank you all again and hope to personally see you at some future date. Please include our unfortunate ancestor into your prayers!

God bless you and our two countries, the sister republics United States of America and Switzerland.

Heinrich L. Wirz
Colonel, Swiss Army
Great-grandnephew of Henry Wirz

The male descendents of Captain Henry Wirz at the Wirz Memorial, 1993. Courtesy of John S. Sims.

Heinrich L. Wirz   10 November 1994 AK/HHW/BM

Forbes Inc.
Forbes Building
60 Fifth Avenue
New York, N.Y. 10011
USA

Civil War Chronicles, Summer 1994, Volume 4/Number 1

Letter to the Editor

"Hell and the Survivor": Camp Sumter Prison, Andersonville, Georgia

Dear Sir

I read with greatest attention this article, an adaptation of the original diary from Charles Ferren Hopkins. For obvious reasons, I am especially interested in all informations on Captain Henry Wirz , A.A.G., C.S.A., my unfortunate great-granduncle from Zurich, Switzerland. He lived in Louisiana and enlisted on 25 May 1861 as Private in Company A, 4th Batallion Louisiana Infantry. He was promoted to Sergeant and—after having been wounded during the battle of Fair Oaks/Seven Pines (near Richmond, VA)—to Captain and Assistant Adjutant General to the staff of John H. Winder , provost marshal general, C.S.A. I do not fundamentally object to such articles. I strongly object to the lack of any critical commentary on the text.

You may say that, as a member of the original Wirz family in Switzerland, I would have no choice, but to defend my ancestor. This is absolutely true after I have thoroughly studied all available materials on Andersonville and its commandant in America and in Europe. All serious historians today speak of Henry Wirz being a 'scapegoat,' the trial being a 'farce,' and the hanging a 'gross injustice.' Major Glen LaForce even writes of a 'national disgrace' (in "The Army Lawyer," June 1988).

Have you ever read the 220 page book *The True Story of Andersonville Prison* by James Madison Page, late 2nd Lieutenant, Company A, Sixth Michigan Cavalry? Why should an officer and prisoner from the Union Army write in favour of the lonely commandant of Camp Sumter Prison?

Do you know the book on Captain Wirz by Jurg Weibel, a Swiss historian? What I am asking for as a non US citizen, but a faithful friend to America, is a balanced and fair review on a subjectively written diary. I hate to read about "Wirz, the helpmate of the devil" or "that human devil, Wirz!" without accurate remarks, based on facts, figures and the desperate situation of the Confederate States in 1864/1865 towards the end of the War of Secession.

I can only hope that one day to come the stain on the name of our family will be taken away by a serious revision of the trial of 1865.

Col. Heinrich L. Wirz

Transcript from a photograph of a typewritten, framed 11/90 - 4/92 copy located in the local museum, Andersonville, GA

CAPTAIN HENRY WIRZ, C.S.A.
Confederate Hero-Martyr

A RESOLUTION PASSED BY
THE GENERAL CONVENTION OF
THE SONS OF CONFEDERATE VETERANS

DALLAS, TEXAS
AUGUST 1977

WHEREAS: The unqualified loyalty of Captain Henry Wirz to his adopted Southland declared by reason of the following facts:

1. He voluntarily enlisted in the 4th Louisiana Infantry in June, 1861;
2. He gave his right arm in the defense of the Confederate capital at the Battle of Seven Pines, 31 May 1862;
3. His manner of performance of duties was such as to earn promotion in the Confederate Service from private to sergeant to captain and Assistant Adjutant General on 12 June 1862 and recommended for Major, which was approved too late in 1865;
4. His important assignments included Assistant Adjutant General in charge of prisons, plenipotentiary of President Davis for special tasks in Paris and Berlin, and for thirteen months the Commandant of the consolidated prison at Andersonville, from 27 March 1864 until paroled with the Army of Tennessee upon the surrender on 26 April 1865;

5. His heroic refusal to plea bargain for his life for his testimony against Jefferson Davis, whose destruction was deeply desired by vindictive radicals.

WHEREAS: The tragic trial of Captain Wirz was unconstitutional in its origin and supremely irregular in its conduct. Note is given to the following: the judgment of Northern historian Bruce Catton, "Wirz was a scapegoat dying for the sins of many, North and South;"
of W.E. Woodward, "His trial was one of the most extraordinary farces that I ever came across;" and of *The National Observer*, in a six column, full page article carrying a handsome portrait of the Confederate Major with a title, "Captain Wirz: 'Confederate Hero-Martyr' (8 November, 1965—the 100th anniversary of Wirz' execution, 10 November 1865.)

THEREFORE BE IT RESOLVED: That this society, the Sons of Confederate Veterans in reunion assembled at Dallas, Texas, does proclaim:

1. That we reciprocate the loyalty of Captain Wirz;
2. That we will know him officially according to the inscription on his grave in Richmond as "Captain Henry Wirz: Confederate Hero-Martyr;"
3. That we will designate the 10th of November each year at 10:32 A.M.—the moment of martyrdom—to be marked in such a manner as a grateful citizenry may choose, calling it HENRY WIRZ MARTYR DAY; and,
4. That we note upon the passage of this resolution that the first "Henry Wirz Martyr Day" will occur on Thursday, 10 November 1977, and it is hoped that as many as can will gather at the Wirz monument in Andersonville at 10:30 A.M. to lay a wreath and do any other appropriate action.

Resolution authored by Arthur Harris Park, Chief of Staff, Florida Division, Sons of Confederate Veterans.

Contemporary Andersonville village.

Site of General Winder's Headquarters in the Village.

Edwin C. Bearss

Chapter Eleven

A Bibliography and Recommended Reading Guide

Edwin C. Bearss, former Chief Historian of the U. S. National Park Service, is nationally known for his work as a Civil War television commentator, author, and lecturer. In 1970, Bearss compiled a detailed study of the Andersonville National Historic Site for the U. S. Department of the Interior's Office of History and Historic Architecture. This publication, now out of print, contains a bibliography and recommended reading guide of note which is reprinted for this particular study; it is a valuable tool for researchers.

BIBLIOGRAPHY

I. PRIMARY SOURCES

Manuscript Materials

Andersonville Letters, Georgia Department of Archives, Atlanta, Georgia.

Claim of Isaac T. Turner, Congressional Jurisdictional Case 11496, National Archives, RG 125.

Collected Confederate Records, Chapter 9, Volume 5, National Archives, RG 109.

Compiled Service Records of Confederate General and Staff Officers and Nonregimented Enlisted Men, National Archives, Microcopy 331.

Compiled Service Records of Confederate Soldiers who Served in Organizations from Florida, National Archives, Microcopy 266.

Compiled Service Records of Confederate Soldiers who Served in Organizations from Georgia, National Archives, Microcopy 266.

Consolidated Correspondence, Office of the Quartermaster General, National Archives, RG 92.

Howell Cobb Letter Books, Cobb Manuscripts, Special Collections Division, University of Georgia Library, Athens, Georgia.

John H. Winder Papers, Southern Historical Society Collections, University of North Carolina, Chapel Hill, North Carolina.

Miscellaneous Records of the Confederate Engineer Department, National Archives, Record Group 109.

Records of the Post Office Department, Records of Appointments of Postmasters, National Archives, RG 28.

Samuel Stout Papers, Southern Historical Society Collection, University of North Carolina, Chapel Hill, North Carolina.

The Harrold Family Papers, Special Collections, Emory University Library, Atlanta, Georgia.

Public Documents

Atwater, Dorence, *A List of Union Soldiers Buried at Andersonville* , New York, 1866.

Narrative of Privations and Suffering, &c. printed for the U.S. Sanitary Commission, Philadelphia, 1864.

Report of the Treatment of Prisoners of War, by the Rebel Authorities, During the War of the Rebellion: to Which Are Appended the Testimony Taken by the Committee, and Official Documents and Statistics, &c., 40th Congress, 3d Session, House Report 45, Washington, 1869.

The Martyrs Who, for Our Country, Gave up Their Lives in the Prison Pens in Andersonville, Ga., Washington, 1866.

The Medical and Surgical History of the War of the Rebellion , six vols., Washington, 1870-1883.

The Trial of Henry Wirz, 40th Congress, 2d Session, House Executive Document 23, Washington, 1868.

County Records

Macon County Deed Books, Macon County Courthouse, Oglethorpe, Georgia.

Sumter County Deed Books, Sumter County Courthouse, Americus, Georgia.

Maps

"Sketch of Andersonville Georgia," National Archives, RG 92.

"Map of the U.S. Prison Park Property, Andersonville, Ga.," to Accompany the Report of E.G. Mitchell, C.E., March 20, 1914, National Archives.

Published Diaries, Reminiscences, and Personal Narratives

Abbott, A.O., *Prison Life in the South: At Richmond, Macon, Savannah, Charleston, Columbia, Charlotte, Raleigh, Goldsborough, and Andersonville, During the Years 1864 and 1865* , New York, 1865.

"Andersonville: Diary of A Prisoner," *The Historical Magazine* , Second Series, Vol. 9, 1871.

Barton, Clara, "Clara Barton to the People of the United States," *New York Tribune*, February 14, 1866.

Boggs, S.S., *Eighteen Months a Prisoner Under the Rebel Flag; A Condensed Pen-Picture of Belle Isle, Danville, Andersonville, Charleston, Florence and Libby Prisons, from Actual Experience*, Lovington, Ill., 1887.

Braun, Herman A., *Andersonville: An Object Lesson on Protection* , Milwaukee, 1892.

Bullard, K.C., *Over the Dead-Line, or Who Killed "Poll Parrot,"* New York, 1909.

Coulter, E. Merton, editor, "From Spotsylvania Courthouse to Andersonville: a Diary of Darius Starr," *Georgia Historical Quarterly*, Vol. 41, 1957.

Creelman, S., *Collections of a Coffee Cooler...* , Wilkinsburg, 1889.

Danker, Donald F., editor, "Imprisoned at Andersonville: The Diary of Albert Harry Shatzel, May 5, 1864-September 12, 1864," *Nebraska History*, Vol. 38, 1958.

Davidson, Henry M., *Experience in Rebel Prisons for United States Soldiers at Richmond, Daqnville, Andersonville, Savannah and Millen*, Cincinnati, 1890.

Davis, S. Boyer, *Escape of a Confederate Officer from Prison; What He Saw at Andersonville; How He Was Sentenced to Death and Saved by the Interposition of President Abraham Lincoln* , Norfolk, 1892.

Day, W.W., *Fifteen Months in Dixie or My Personal Experience in Rebel Prisons*, Owatonna 1889.

Destler, Chester M., editor, "A Vermonter in Andersonville: Diary of Charles Ross, 1864," *Vermont History,* Vol. 25, 1957.

Forbes, Eugene, *Diary of a Soldier, and Prisoner of War in Rebel Prisons,* Trenton, 1865.

Glazier, Willard W., *The Capture, the Prison Pen, and the Escape: Giving a Complete History of Prison Life in the South... "* New York, 1870.

Goss, Warren L., *The Soldier's Story of His Captivity at Andersonville, Belle Isle, and Other Rebel Prisons,* Boston, 1868.

Isham, Asa B., Henry M. Davidson, and Henry B. Furness, *Prisoners of War and Military Prisons; Personal Narratives of Experience in the Prisons at Richmond, Danville, Macon, Andersonville, Savannah, Millen, Charleston, and Columbia, With a General Account of Prison Life and Prisons in the South During the War of the Rebellion, Including Statistical Information Pertaining to Prisoners of War, Together with a List of Officers Who Were Prisoners of War from January 1, 1864,* Cincinnati, 1890.

Jones, J.B., *A Rebel Clerk's Diary,* New York, 1935.

Kellogg, Robert H., *Life and Death in Rebel Prisons: Giving a Complete History of the Inhuman and Barbarous Treatment of our Brave Soldiers by Rebel Authorities, Inflicting Terrible Suffering and Frightful Mortality, Principally at Andersonville, Ga., and Florence, S.C., Describing Plans of Escape, Arrival of Prisoners, with Numerous and Varied Incidents and Anecdotes of Prison Life,* Hartford, 1865.

Lightcap, William H., *The Horrors of Southern Prisons During the War of the Rebellion,* Platteville, Wis., 1902.

Long, Lessel, *Twelve Months in Andersonville, On the March-In the Battle - In the Rebel Prison Pens, and at Last in God's Country ,* Huntington, Ind., 1896.

Lyon, William F., *In and Out of Andersonville Prison ,* Detroit, 1907.

Maile, John L., *Prison Life in Andersonville,* Chicago, 1912.

Mann, T.H., "A Yankee in Andersonville," *The Century Magazine,* Vol. 18, 1890.

McElroy, John, *Andersonville: A Story of Rebel Military Prisons; Fifteen Months a Guest of the So-called Southern Confederacy A Private Soldier's Experience in Richmond, Andersonville, Savannah, Millen, Blackshear and Florence*, Toledo, 1879.

Northrop, John W., *Chronicles from the Diary of a War Prisoner in Andersonville and Other Prisons of the South in 1864*, Wichita, 1904.

O'Dea, Thomas, *History of O'Dea's Famous Picture of Andersonville Prison*, Cohoes, 1887.

Ransom, John L., *Andersonville Diary, Escape, and List of the Dead, With Name, Col, Regiment, Date of Death and No. of Grave in Cemetery*, Auburn, 1881.

Roe, Alfred S., *The Melvin Memorial, Sleepy Hollow Cemetery, Concord, Massachusetts; A Brother's Tribute; Exercises at Dedication, June 16, 1909*, Cambridge, 1910.

Sabre, G.E., *Nineteen Months a Prisoner of War; Narrative of Lieutenant G. E. Sabre, Second Rhode Island Cavalry Of His Experience in the War Prisons and Stockades of Morton, Mobile, Atlanta, Libby, Belle Island, Andersonville, Macon, Charleston, and Columbia, During the Wintyer of 1864 and 1865*, New York, 1865.

Spencer, Ambrose, *A Narrative of Andersonville, Drawn from the Evidence Elicited on The Trial of Henry Wirz the Jailer; with the Argument of Col. N.P. Chipman, Judge Advocate*, New York, 1866.

Urban, John W., *In Defense of the Union; Or Through Shot and Shell and Prison Pen*, Chicago, 1887.

Vaughter, John B., *Prison Life in Dixie*, Chicago, 1880.

Unpublished Diaries and Reminiscences

Kennedy, David, "Diary," transcript, Minnesota Historical Society, St. Paul, Minnesota.

Reminiscences of J.M. Ball, 3d Georgia Reserves, "Reminiscences of Confederate Soldiers," U.D.C., Georgia State Archives, Atlanta, Georgia.

Reminiscences of William D. Hammack, Company G 55th Georgia, U.D.C., "Reminiscences of Confederate Soldiers," Georgia State Archives, Atlanta Georgia.

II.   SECONDARY SOURCES

Biographies

Barton, William E., *The Life of Clara Barton: Founder of the American Red Cross*, 2 volumes, Boston, 1922.

Williams, Blanche Colton, *Clara Barton: Daughter of Destiny*, New York, 1914.

Travel Accounts

Ball, J.L., to Rich and Maris, *West Branch Local Record*, March 10, 1881.

Gue, Benjamin F., "The Story of Andersonville," reprinted in *The Palimpsest*, Vol. 47, Iowa City, Iowa.

Shearman, Mary A., "A Visit to Andersonville," *Hours at Home: A Popular Monthly, Devoted to Religious and Useful Literature* , New York, 1867, Vol. 5.

Trowbridge, J.T., *The South: A Tour of Its Battlefields and Ruined Cities*, Hartford, 1866.

Trowbridge, John T., *The Desolate South, 1865-1866*, edited by Gordon Carroll, Boston, 1956.

"W.D.," *Boston Spectator & Weekly Advertiser* , April 9, 1868.

Webster, Albert, "A Jaunt in the South," *Appleton's Journal*, Vol. 10.

Monographs

Davis, Jefferson, *Andersonville and Other War Prisons* , New York, 1890.

Futch, Ovid, *History of Andersonville Prison* , Gainesville, 1968.

Hamlin, Augustus C., *Martyria; or Andersonville Prison* , Boston, 1866.

Hesseltine, William B., *Civil War Prisons: A Study in War Psychology* , New York, 1964.

Jones, Joseph, *Medical and Surgical Memoirs: containing Investigations on the Geographical Distribution, Causes, Nature, Relations and Treatment of Various Diseases, 1855-1890* , New Orleans, 1890.

Richardson, Rufus B., "Andersonville," *The New Englander*, Vol. 3, 1880.

Stibbs, John H., "Andersonville and the Trial of Henry Wirz," *The Iowa Journal of History and Politics* , Vol. 9, 1911.

Tyler, Lyon G., "Major Henry Wirz," *The William and Mary College Quarterly*, Vol. 27, 1919.

Reports of State Commissions and Histories of the Prison Pen

Averill, James P., *Andersonville Prison Park*, Atlanta, 1898.

Commonwealth of Massachusetts, Report of Commission on Andersonville Monument, Boston, 1902.

Dedication of the Monument at Andersonville, Georgia, October 23, 1907, in Memory of the Men of Connecticut who Suffered in Southern Military Prisons, 1861-1865 , Hartford, 1908.

Elarton, J.W., *Andersonville Prison and National Cemetery, Andersonville, Georgia*, Aurora, 1913.

Report of the Joint Committee on Erection of Rhode Island Monument at Andersonville, Ga., Providence, 1903.

Novels

Kantor, MacKinley, *Andersonville*, New York, 1955.
[Editor's note: this work of fiction contains an excellent bibliographical section.]

Mauriel Joslyn

Epilogue
Who Caused Andersonville?

Mauriel Joslyn, a Civil War POW historian and author, lives in Sparta, Georgia.

In our western culture, there has always been an unwritten law for the treatment of captives in military situations. In the 1400s, the Chivalric Code stipulated that a knight captured in battle was to be treated respectfully as an unarmed and defenseless prisoner, and his captor was responsible for him. He was to receive the same food, shelter, and protection as his captors. It was a code of honor, and strictly forbidden was any mistreatment of prisoners. A knight was given a ransom, a value set on his head to be paid by his king. If he could not raise this ransom, then he could call for a substitute to take his place in prison. So honorable was this system, that during the Hundred Years War between England and France, the French king was captured and confined in London. He was able to gain his freedom by sending his son to sit out his prison term, and he maintained his role as ruler while the wars continued.

Through the centuries, this same code of honor continued to be the accepted treatment. It was in keeping with the strong principles of Christianity practiced by Western nations, who prided themselves on their civilized behavior in comparison with the cultures of the East, which were seen as barbarous and ruthless.

By the time of the American Revolution, the ransom had been abolished, and captives were simply held until the end of the war. However, a complicating factor arose during this war. The American colonists distinctly saw themselves as fighting for independence. The British Crown saw them as traitors in rebellion. While the colonists called for humane treatment of British soldiers captured in battle, the British adopted a policy of harshness, declaring captives outlaws, and executing them under British laws dealing with deserters. The recognition of American soldiers as legitimate prisoners of war was not adopted until 1782, a year before the war ended. Before that time, the American Congress adopted retaliation on British soldiers, in other words to treat captives as American soldiers were treated. They did not go so far as to execute men, but rather confined them in the same conditions on board prison ships, with poor food and no medical care. Hundreds of British soldiers died, and finally a treaty was struck. So a new era in history put a dent in the old Chivalric Code of the Middle Ages. Though the American government had set out with honorable treatment, it succumbed to using reprisals as a means of securing better treatment for American soldiers in British hands.

Both sides were shocked at what they had inflicted on helpless men, and in 1785, hoping to prevent such treatment ever again, the United States and Prussia signed what was the earliest formal agreement on the treatment of prisoners of war. It stipulated that men would not be confined in unhealthy conditions nor denied proper life sustaining necessities. It was the forerunner to the modern day Geneva Convention, and was the only document in effect during WWI.

Subsequent wars were much the same story. The War of 1812 saw no neglect of prisoners, because both sides saw them as legitimate prisoners of war, and not traitors. A cartel was agreed upon which provided for the exchange of prisoners, known as the Winder Cartel, in 1814. The Mexican War was also generally humane on captives. Most were released on parole and allowed to return home. The Mexican government reciprocated with its captives, and both sides maintained a record they could be proud of in regard to prisoners of war.

All that would change with the War Between the States. And I can prepare you for the details by saying that it may be considered the first modern war technologically, but it regressed regarding the treatment of prisoners of war. It was the worst record in United States history, and broke every rule in the book prior to or since the war. The old Chivalric Code bit the dust.

At first, the United States adhered to the policy adopted in the 1780s. "Prisoners of war are to be considered as unfortunate and not as criminal, and are to be treated accordingly, although the question of detention or liberation is one affecting the interest of the captor alone. [This] by no means implies the right to dispose of the prisoners at the pleasure of the captor. That right involves certain duties, among them that of providing the prisoners with the necessaries of Life and abstaining from the infliction of any punishment upon them..."

Early in 1861, the Confederate Congress passed a stipulation that provided the same humane protection for prisoners of war. Actually, the U.S. Congress had never passed such a law—it only had international agreements, not laws.

Remember what I said about the British perception that the Americans were rebels and not fighting for independence? In 1861, the United States took the old British position, and saw the Confederacy in the same way—as traitors. Lincoln refused to admit the "right of a state to secede," and therefore Southern soldiers were "insurgents" and her sailors labeled "pirates." The very terminology paved the way for the justifiable abuse of prisoners of war.

The first incident involving captured Southerners concerned twelve sailors imprisoned in a dungeon known as "The Tombs" in New York in June 1861. The men were sentenced to be hung. The Confederate government was outraged, and vowed to do the same with any Northerners captured. When the British government issued a condemnation of Union action, Northern sentiment backed down and Lincoln had to retract part of his determination to mistreat prisoners.

When it became apparent after the Battle of First Manassas that this would be a bloody conflict lasting longer than 30 days, Lincoln was forced to make a decision about how to treat prisoners of war. The South held the greater number of captives, and public sentiment in the North clamored for some agreement to release prisoners. The old Winder cartel from the War of 1812 was resurrected and rehashed to try and uphold Lincoln's refusal to recognize the South as a legitimate nation. Lincoln appointed Gen. John Dix as a representative to meet with Confederate authorities and try to work out an agreement. On July 22, 1862, Dix met with Confederate Gen. Daniel Harvey Hill, and the Dix-Hill cartel came into effect. This ingenious document designated a value system for exchanging men and officers held as prisoners of war. For instance, officers could be exchanged grade for grade, or a general equaled 60 privates; a major was worth 8 privates, and privates were exchanged man for man. With an incredible premonition of things to come, the stipulation was added by Dix and Hill that this cartel would bind both sides to continue exchanges, even if disputes over the exact terms occurred in the future. Disputes most definitely occurred.

To carry out the terms of the cartel, each side appointed an agent of exchange. This agent would be responsible for getting the rolls of prisoners names, seeing that the correct number of men were taken to the place of exchange, and check the rolls of the men he was receiving for his government to make sure the correct number were given him. The first months of the cartel saw every prisoner of war exchanged, and the prisons emptied by September 1862. After leaving prison the system provided for the parole of a prisoner. He would spend this time of limbo between release and official exchange at home, on his honor not to return to the army until he was officially notified that the man released in his place was exchanged. Then he would be declared officially exchanged, and could return to his regiment to fight again. One major factor that caused the North to break the terms of the cartel had to do with this return to duty. For many soldiers in the Union army, their terms of enlistment were up. They didn't go back to their regiments because they didn't want to reinlist. On the other hand, nearly every Confederate soldier returned to the ranks immediately. U.S. Secretary of War Edwin M. Stanton even accused Union soldiers of getting captured deliberately so they could either get exchanged and go home or spend time in the safety of prison rather than risk their lives on the battlefield.

When Lincoln was notified of this, he decided the North was not getting any benefit from exchanging prisoners, and declared the Dix-Hill cartel void. The north cancelled any more exchanges of Confederate officers. However, special exchanges of enlisted men continued due to the dedication of the exchange agents, who truly wanted to do what was best for prisoners of both sides. Lincoln still sought some way to justify his attitude that the South should not be treated as a legitimate nation.

In January 1863, Lincoln further complicated the lives of prisoners of war by issuing the Emancipation Proclamation. For the North this document adopted the goal of freeing the slaves as further incentive to stay at war. For the South, it changed the status of blacks fighting as soldiers.

Previously, both sides had agreed that any black captured in uniform, if he had been a slave before enlistment, was to be returned to his owner as property. The North now demanded that blacks captured by the South were entitled to the same treatment as all prisoners of war, and exchanged. The Confederate Congress debated the issue the winter of 1863, and though they agreed that free blacks captured would continue to be treated the same as white prisoners of war, former slaves did not demand the same treatment, because they were classified as property. This issue became the pivot upon which the whole exchange question turned. It was not a popular decision in the North, where citizens were finding more and more reasons not to support the war, and Lincoln was losing popularity.

Lincoln was walking a fine line to justify his stance not to adhere to the cartel until all blacks were exchanged. He had to find a way to manipulate the laws of war to support his policy. So he sought the advice of Francis Lieber to recodify the laws of war to fit his policy of not exchanging prisoners of war. Francis Lieber was a very liberal law professor, who came to South Carolina from Prussia in the 1840s. In 1861, he was a professor at Columbia University in New York. He was a strong supporter of the Constitution, and the rights of the individual. He came up with what has become known to history as the Lieber Code. This was a humanitarian document defining the rules for treatment of prisoners of war, but based on precedents which involved neither recognition of the South, nor foregoing the right to try them for treason after the war. Though it contains contradictions and reflects the nature of a fratricidal conflict, it is recognized as the first concept of a written international policy pertaining to the disposition of prisoners of war. Lieber had sons fighting on both sides in the War Between the States, and had every right to favor exchange, yet he was a strong advocate for the preservation of the Union.

In July 1863, the Battles of Gettysburg and Vicksburg, and the surrender of the Port Hudson garrison in Louisiana were to have a devastating impact on the Southerners captured at those places. The North was inconsistent on its own policies. Grant was allowed to exchange the 20,000 Vicksburg captives, but Union Gen. Nathaniel Banks was not allowed to parole the Port Hudson garrison of 4,000. These men would spend the next two years in military prisons in the North. Lincoln for the first time had more prisoners than the South had, and decided to withhold the South's manpower by not allowing any more exchanges of prisoners of war. He used the argument that it was because the South refused to exchange all black soldiers. His exchange agent, Gen. Benjamin Butler admitted that this was only an excuse to the public in order to cancel exchange. Butler was in favor of exchange, because all the soldiers in Southern prisons could be freed, while still withholding 13,000 Southerners from returning to the Confederate army. However, Gen. Ulysses S. Grant intervened and convinced Lincoln not to exchange any more men. Union soldiers were still not reinlisting, while Southerners reinforced Gen. Robert E. Lee's army daily. "It is preferable to feed prisoners rather than fight soldiers" was his motto. Oddly enough, 1864 was the first year that the Geneva Convention met in Geneva, Switzerland. Its goal was to alleviate the conditions of fighting men and prisoners of war, based on the findings of Florence Nightingale during the Crimean War. The United States sent a delegate, but refrained from joining.

Therefore, despite the fact that the Confederate Congress agreed in August 1864 to exchanging all blacks captured in uniform, no more prisoners were to be freed.

What did this do to the man who found himself a prisoner of war? These factors directly caused the overcrowding in prisons of both sides, designed to hold only a few thousand men at a time. For the North, the resources were plentiful for feeding and clothing prisoners. Though crowded, Confederate soldiers were given necessities, and medical care was provided. However, by 1864 in the South, resources were being stretched to a breaking point. The soldier in the field was being deprived of the basic necessities of clothing and food due to the blockade. Union authorities declared any medicine captured on blockade runners contraband, therefore denying medical treatment not only to the Confederate Army, but the men confined in Southern prisons as well. So Union soldiers suffered. The concept of total war, introduced by Gen. William T. Sherman in the Summer and Fall of 1864 destroyed resources on the homefront. Transportation and communication lines were disrupted, thereby making it impossible to transport food and provisions to any parts of the South. This affected the military prisons as well, especially the thousands of men confined at Andersonville.

What is worthy of our attention is how the prisoners coped. The hardships and terrible conditions are something we can hardly envision today. I know 20th century wars have had their own notorious brand of treatment of POWs, such as the Bataan Death March during WWII. But it is truly one of the most admirable examples of behavior to read how some of the soldiers of both sides survived imprisonment during the War Between the States.

The details of the conditions at Andersonville are pretty well known. It was only in operation from February 1864 until September 1865, when most of the men were removed to Charleston and Savannah where they could receive food and medical treatment. It comprised 26 acres surrounded by a high stockade fence. The prison commandant was Capt. Henry Wirz, a Swiss doctor. He had plans to build barracks buildings, but could not get enough lumber. Because the North cancelled exchange, the prison became crowded with new captives from the 1864 battles in Virginia. By August nearly 33,000 men were crowded into the stockade, and facilities for sanitation were inadequate. Food shortages occurred and scurvy was rampant. Most Union soldiers recorded an understanding of the conditions and mention that the guards were as generous as possible, often sharing their own rations with prisoners. They never directly blamed the Confederate government, but realized it was their own government that kept them in these conditions by not reinstating exchange.

At all prisons, North and South, the guard troops varied in attitude. There are always going to be some who resent enemy soldiers, and show no sympathy. But on the whole there were kind guards to be found. You can't make a sweeping statement about individual attitudes, that they were all good or all bad. That's not true today.

The Confederate soldiers in Northern prisons, who were deprived of food and shelter on purpose, suffered from exposure to the severe winter. The winter of 1864-65 was one of the worst on record for the 19th century. At Johnson's Island in Ohio, it was 40 below zero, and many Confederate officers had no blanket. Many froze to death. The overall commander of the Federal military prisons in Maryland and Delaware was so frugal with funds provided to buy vegetables and medical supplies that he returned $2 million to the U.S. Treasury, saying it was not needed, while thousands of Confederate soldiers starved to death.

Prison life was an emotionally battering experience. The men lived with uncertainty every day, not knowing when they would be released. Monotony, hunger, fear, and sickness all vied for a hold on the men's spirits. These conditions were endured in many ways. Religion played a very large part of everyday life. It provided hope, and Bible study was a source of comparison for the soldiers' own circumstances with those of prophets and disciples who were rewarded for their suffering.

A major pastime was writing to loved ones at home, and the letters received in return were spiritual food. It kept them going, and gave them a reason to live. Northern prisons occasionally would withhold mail, and this was dreadful punishment to the men.

On lighter notes, gambling was well established. Certain barracks became regular business casinos. Talented men set up shop as barbers, jewelers, or artists. A community spirit existed at most prisons, and even an economy maintained by the funds cleverly hidden from authorities or smuggled in by "fresh fish," or new arrivals. When funds were not sufficient, a barter system was put into effect. Teachers held classes, dance lessons were given, and even a debating society or theatre group established. For those more adventurous men, escape attempts took up a considerable amount of time, and were occasionally successful.

The Confederate authorities were well aware of the situations in the military prisons, and pleaded on humanitarian grounds that exchange be reinstated. Over 13,000 prisoners were released and sent to Union authorities without demanding any Southern soldiers in exchange, simply to release the prisoners so that they did not cause a drain on the resources of the South. A delegation was paroled and sent from Andersonville to Washington, comprised of Union officers confined there, to convince Lincoln that they were suffering and that only exchange would alleviate the suffering. Lincoln refused to see the men.

As stories of starvation and lack of necessary clothing and shelter began to leak out, citizens in the North were deliberately misled into thinking the South was mistreating prisoners of war on purpose. The passions this raised gained public support for the war, and people demanded measures to force the South to stop mistreatment or either return to exchange.

Instead, the North adopted the policy of Retaliation on Rebel Prisoners of War. This debate went on for three months, and resulted in the passage of HR 97, whereby "Rebel prisoners in our hands are to be subjected to a treatment finding its parallels only in the conduct of savage tribes and resulting in the death of multitudes by the slow but designed process of starvation and by mortal diseases occasioned by insufficient and unhealthy food and wanton exposure of their persons to the inclemency of the weather." This is a direct quote from the preamble to the resolution. Though moderate senators, and even Francis Lieber himself, argued against it, declaring it legal murder of prisoners of war, it passed, and was put into effect. Thousands of Southerners died in Northern prisons simply because the North chose not to provide the necessities of life. Upon learning of the conditions of Confederate soldiers in Northern prisons, a British aid society sent a ship to Philadelphia, loaded with over $8,000 worth of clothing, blankets and medicines. It was not allowed to dock. Men starved to death in a land of plenty. The policy of retaliation caused Southern soldiers to be placed under fire of their own guns to protect Union batteries in the siege of Charleston, a situation directly condemned by the international laws of war. This revenge did not save a single soldier confined at Andersonville, or any other Southern prison. Rather it added to their hardships. Only exchange would have saved their lives, and the Lincoln administration refused.

After the war, a Union officer confined at Andersonville named Edward Wellington Boate summed up the feelings of many of the soldiers he shared confinement with when he wrote:

"A policy like this is the quintessence of inhumanity, a disgrace to the Administration which carried it out, and a blot upon the country. You rulers who make the charge that the rebels intentionally killed off our men, when I can honestly swear they were doing every thing in their power to sustain us, do not lay this flattering unction to your souls. You abandoned your brave men in the hour of their cruelest need. They fought for the Union, and you reached no hand out to save the old faithful, loyal, and devoted servants of the country. You may try to shift the blame from your own shoulders, but posterity will saddle the responsibility where it justly belongs."

Let's hope that the truth of Andersonville will one day be admitted. It was the result of letting a political agenda take precedence over reason and humanitarianism—to win at all costs. Until that admission comes, it is a blot on the pages of the history of this nation—not because of *what* happened there, but *why.*

American POW's of all wars are honored by the
Georgia Monument at Andersonville National Cemetery.